To Mel with love
from E.J. & Evelyn
Christmas 1993

Pig Boats and River Hogs
Further Voyages into Michigan's Past

Pontiac inciting his warriors to "take up the hatchet" as depicted in an 1863 steel engraving.

Pig Boats and River Hogs
Further Voyages into Michigan's Past

By

Larry B. Massie

The Priscilla Press
Allegan Forest, Michigan
1990

Cover by Diane Tedora

ISBN-0-9626408-0-8
First Edition - May 1990

For Priscilla, who makes my dreams come true.

TABLE OF CONTENTS

Preface

Welcome to *Pig Boats and River Hogs,* the third volume of my *Voyages into Michigan's Past* series.

Once again we will explore the length and breadth of these two great peninsulas in quest of colorful historical episodes - the human interest stories that glitter across the richly woven tapestry which is Michigan's past.

We will paddle in a birch-bark bateau with Father Marquette and his hardy voyageurs; duck our heads under low bridges with pioneer immigrants journeying westward on the Erie Canal; tramp across the Lower Peninsula with Nessmuk, a sportsman far ahead of his time; walk up the gang plank of the Walk-in-the-Water, the Philo Parsons and the ill-fated Chicora; battle the monster waves heaved up by the Big Blow of 1913; accompany Art and Aimee Smith on their 1912 elopement in a biplane and experience the horrors of the fiery holocaust at Metz.

We will stop off at ghost towns like Fayette and Port Sheldon and tour Michigan's insular jewels including Mackinac, Grand, Drummond and Isle Royale.

We will lay in ambush with Charles de Langlade, the Michilimackinac-born terror of the frontier; relive the River Raisin massacre; survive the shot and shell of Civil War battles; tunnel out of Libby Prison and go over the top with the gallant men of the Red Arrow Division.

Perhaps most importantly, we will make some mighty interesting acquaintances in our travels. We will get to know Indian chiefs Waukazoo and Pontiac, and writers Ring Lardner, David Grayson and L. Frank Baum, the man who gave the world the Wizard of Oz. We will chat with women who made their mark on Michigan history — Laura Haviland, Pauline Cushman, Anna Howard Shaw and Caroline Bartlett Crane. And you can count on meeting some never-to-be-forgotten eccentrics including Lyman F. Stowe, who predicted Detroit's future; Daniel B. Kellogg, Ann Arbor's clairvoyant physician; and Dr. Thomas Sheldon Andrews, the celebrated matchmaking phrenologist.

These essays originally appeared in the *Kalamazoo Gazette, Grand Rapids Press, Muskegon Chronicle* and *Saginaw News*. I have restored text that was deleted in some newspapers because of space limitations, corrected errors that came to my attention following the article's original publication and added a bibliography to facilitate further research.

I have taken my porcine title from chapter 30 which deals with whaleback freighters, popularly known as pig boats, and chapter 31 about the adventures of a young river hog, as those daring loggers who rode the cork pine downstream to the booming grounds were called. The cover illustration represents Marquette artist Diane Tedora's conception of the Christopher Columbus, a whaleback passenger vessel which carried millions of excursionists as it plied the waters of Lake Michigan for more the 40 years.

For valuable research assistance I am indebted to Dr. LeRoy Barnett, Geneva Wiskemann and Dick Kishbaum. Al Beet accomplished masterful photographic processing. Dave Person's superb editing skills were much appreciated. Jim Mosby and Mary Kramer of the *Kalamazoo Gazette*, Ray Kwapil of the *Grand Rapids Press*, Gunnar Carlson, editor of the *Muskegon Chronicle*, and Paul Chaffee, editor of the *Saginaw News* were particularly supportive during the third year of my weekly Michigan history series. Judy Barz and Dena Haffner of *The Auction Exchange* located in Plainwell, Michigan, produced the camera ready copy.

My wife, friend and partner, Priscilla, constantly inspired me, converted my hen scratching into typed copy and performed the copy stand photographic work.

This volume marks the first product of the Priscilla Press. It will be distributed in cooperation with Avery Color Studios of Au Train, Michigan, those good folks from the U. P. who produced the preceding two volumes in the *Voyages into Michigan's Past* series.

Larry B. Massie
Allegan Forest

The Missionary with the Heart of an Explorer

Father Marquette receiving geography lessons from the Indians at St. Ignace, as drawn by Father Edward Jacker in the 1870's.

The frail birch-bark canoe glided down the fabled Mississippi River in June 1673. Each bend revealed vistas perhaps never before seen by white men. For Father Jacques Marquette, it was a long-cherished dream come true.

At Lake Michigan's Green Bay, where he had left the known world a few weeks earlier, the Indians had warned him of the dangers he would face should he continue his mission to explore the length of the Mississippi. They told him he "would meet nations that never spare strangers but tomahawk them without any provocation," and the "Great River" was "full of frightful monsters who swallowed up men and canoes together." The black-robed priest had replied that to save the souls of those he sought, "I would be happy to lay down my life."

While but a lad in his native Laon, France, Marquette had thirsted for missionary work in some exotic land. Undoubtedly, he had read some of the annual volumes of the Jesuit Relations, which beginning in 1632 had thrilled France with accounts of the bravery and martyrdom of those Jesuits who carried the cross to the new world. At the age of 17, Marquette had joined the Jesuit order. After two years as a novitiate, he took the vows of poverty, chastity, and obedience.

Next came 10 long years of study and teaching, for which he held little aptitude, while he repeatedly beseeched his superiors to grant him a post in a foreign mission. Finally, in 1666, the 29-year-old priest was assigned to New France. At Three Rivers, 80 miles west of Quebec, he studied Indian languages under the guidance of the veteran missionary, Father Gabriel Druillettes. He showed particular aptitude, learning Algonquin, Huron, Iroquois, and Montagnais in two years time and later two additional dialects.

In 1668, Marquette was assigned to the mission at Sault Ste. Marie, and the following year, he was chosen to replace Father Claude Allouez at the Mission Saint Esprit on Chequamegon Bay near present-day Ashland, Wisconsin. He found the Chippewa there friendly but loath to relinquish their native religion. Even after apparent conversion and baptism, they had the disturbing habit of reverting to their former beliefs, which featured many "manitous," idols, and witch doctors. Marquette found, however, the baptism of those who were dying, a "surer harvest."

While at Chequamegon Bay, he encountered some Illinois Indians who had journeyed there to trade. They seemed more eager to accept Christianity. Marquette began studying their language in preparation for his goal of establishing a mission in their country to the south. From the Illinois, he first learned of a great river which they had crossed during their trek to the north. It was "nearly a league in width, flows from north to south, and to such a distance that the Illinois have not yet heard of any mention of its mouth." Marquette suspected that the river might be the long-sought water route to California.

In 1670, war erupted between the Huron and Ottawa, who lived along the south shore of Lake Superior, and the Sioux. Marquette convinced a large contingent of his charges to migrate east to escape the wrath of the Sioux. In the spring of 1671, a flotilla of canoes laden with Indian families and all their household goods slowly made its way along the south shore of Lake Superior. The Ottawa returned to Manitoulin Island, their ancestral homeland, while a group of Hurons established a new abode on Mackinac Island, selected for its defensive potential.

Father Claude Dablon had previously established a primitive mission near the southern tip of the island, and he assigned Marquette there.

It did not prosper, however, largely because the thin layer of soil that covered bedrock proved unsuitable for raising corn. Accordingly, sometime in the early fall of 1671, Marquette and his flock moved the mission site to present-day Saint Ignace. There they erected a chapel and

15

village surrounded by a palisaded fort.

Marquette's labors in converting the Indians at St. Ignace and keeping them converted were interrupted during the winter of 1672 by the arrival of a 22-year-old voyageur named Louis Jolliet. He had been commissioned by the ambitious intendant of New France, Jean Talon, to explore the "great river of the west" in quest of a water route to the Pacific Ocean. Marquette's heart sang when he learned that he was to accompany Jolliet.

During the succeeding winter and spring, Marquette and Jolliet carefully planned the adventure. Marquette gathered from the Indians information on the geography of the west, and he sketched a rudimentary map of the proposed route.

On the morning of May 17, 1673, Marquette, Jolliet, and five voyageurs pushed off from St. Ignace in two light canoes. Their only provisions were Indian corn and jerky. They made their "paddles play merrily" as they cruised the northern shore of "Lac de Illinois" as Lake Michigan was then known. Stopping briefly at the mouth of the Menominee River, they encountered a tribe known as the "people of the wild oats" because they subsisted largely on the wild rice that grew there. It was the "wild oats" who warned Marquette of the horrors he would face on the great river.

Nevertheless, the explorers pushed on, up the rapids-filled Lower Fox River to Lake Winnebago, then 50 miles up the Upper Fox River to a large Indian village where they made a portage to the Wisconsin River. On June 17, 1673, "with a joy I cannot express," Marquette reached the Mississippi.

The French did indeed discover monsters on the river. Once, a gigantic catfish struck Marquette's canoe with such force that he thought he had hit a log. As they paddled down the river, they observed other strange animals on shore, including the first buffalo to be described by a Frenchman. But for nearly 300 miles, they saw no sign of human life.

16

Then one day Marquette spied footprints on the muddy shore that led to a well-beaten path. Following that path, the explorers came upon a large village. Fortunately, the inhabitants proved friendly. The peace pipe was passed, and the Indians killed and boiled a dog for the ceremonial feast.

The French experienced many other adventures before reaching the mouth of the Arkansas River. Having satisfied themselves that the Mississippi River did not flow into the Pacific and fearing capture by the hostile Spanish should they proceed south, the explorers began their return journey on July 17. They took a different route in returning to Green Bay, traveling up the Illinois River to Lake Michigan.

Marquette stayed at Green Bay, intending to return to missionary work in the Illinois country. Jolliet paddled back to Quebec to report his discoveries. Unfortunately, his canoe overturned in the rapids below the city, and his journal and maps were lost. However, Marquette's account of the expedition was eventually published in 1681.

Weakened by the hardships of his journey, Marquette developed a case of dysentery. He recovered enough to make another journey to the Illinois country in 1674. He remained there during the winter of 1674/75, but he suffered a relapse of dysentery.

He set out with two companions shortly after Easter, 1675, in an attempt to reach his beloved mission at St. Ignace before he died. But he grew weaker en route, and knowing his end was near, he asked to be put ashore at the mouth of the river that was later named in his honor near present-day Ludington. He died a few hours later and, as had been his request, he was buried atop a nearby sand hill.

Two years later, a band of Ottawa dug up his body, removed the flesh from the bones as was their custom, and transported the bones to St. Ignace. They were buried in the chapel there, which was abandoned a few decades later.

Father Edward Jacker rediscovered fragments of Mar-

17

quette's bones in 1877. Some of those precious relics were reburied beneath the monument to his memory erected at St. Ignace, and the remainder are now at Marquette University in Milwaukee. A campaign is currently under way to have Father Marquette declared a saint.

Supposed portrait of Father Marquette.

Chief Pontiac and the Mysterious Blabber

One of the many artists' renditions of Catherine spilling the beans to Major Gladwin.

Chief Pontiac stomped his moccasined foot in fury, then kicked a nearby campfire, sending burning brands in every direction. His rage was that of "a lioness robbed of all her whelps."

Pontiac, a brilliant Ottawa chief who had linked the tribes of Michigan and border regions into a confederacy intent on driving the British from their domain, had been betrayed. His crafty plan to massacre the garrison at Fort Detroit had failed ingloriously. Moreover, he had suffered humiliation from the British commander, Maj. Henry Gladwin. There was only one explanation for the debacle—someone had blabbed.

It was May 8, 1763. The bloody French and Indian War, in which the western tribes had allied themselves with the French, had ended in a complete British victory. Into British hands passed all territory the French had claimed east of the Mississippi River.

While the French had traditionally cultivated rapport with the Indians, the incoming British were arrogant, imperious, and tight-fisted in their trading policies. What is more, the Indians resented the fact that their homelands had been signed away by one king to another without their compliance.

Pontiac, who was born in the Detroit vicinity, probably in 1720, began to plot their demise soon after the British garrison arrived there. As more and more soldiers and traders streamed into Michigan, Pontiac realized he needed to strike quickly. His leadership would inspire "the most formidable Indian resistance that the English-speaking people had ever faced."

Whether he actually controlled the entire Indian campaign of 1763 that resulted in the loss of all Great Lakes posts with the exception of Detroit is open to debate. But one thing is certain, Detroit was the first to be attacked, and Pontiac was the brains behind that operation.

During a grand council meeting held at the mouth of the Ecorse River downstream from Detroit on April 27, 1763,

Pontiac's brilliant oratory convinced the 460 Potawatomi, Ottawa, and Huron warriors in attendance to go on the warpath.

On May 1, the British first noticed an increase in population at the three Indian villages located near Detroit. That afternoon, also, Pontiac and 40 or 50 of his most trusted warriors appeared at the fort to perform a ceremonial dance in Gladwin's honor. Their actual purpose was to spy out the strength of the garrison and locate the various supplies they planned on plundering.

As Pontiac and most of the warriors performed the calumet dance, 10 of their number drifted into the crowd to accomplish their reconnaissance of the fort. When the dance ended, Pontiac told Gladwin he would return with more of his people in a few days for a formal parley.

By May 4, the Indians had borrowed files from some of the French habitants with which they began to saw off the ends of their muskets. Pontiac revealed the rest of his plan to the assembled warriors during a war council held at the Potawatomi village south of the fort the following afternoon. To safeguard the conspiracy, Pontiac ordered all the women removed from the village, and he stationed guards around its periphery.

Then he outlined his scheme. With tomahawks, scalping knives, and sawed-off muskets concealed under their blankets, Pontiac and 60 of his best warriors would enter the fort and seek a council with Gladwin. The rest of the Ottawa would also enter the fort, thusly armed, and, at a given signal, all would commence slaughtering the unsuspecting garrison. The signal, depending on whose version you choose to believe, was either a war whoop or the reversal of a wampum belt.

Pontiac's clever plan might well have worked—had not someone blabbed. By the evening of May 7, Gladwin knew all about the plot. Who had informed him remains one of the unsolved mysteries of Michigan history.

Several leading historians, including the great Francis

Parkman, accepted the version that Gladwin had been personally warned by a beautiful young squaw named Catherine who was in love with him. Numerous old paintings and prints depict the comely maiden, a la Pocahontas, in the act of spilling the beans. Another version, however, has Catherine as a wrinkled old hag who betrayed her people for a dram of whiskey.

Various others have also vied for the title "savior of Detroit" ranging from a certain Angelique Cuillerier, a pretty French damsel who later married James Sterling, a Scotch trader in residence at Detroit, to the daughter of an interpreter named LaButte, to a Mrs. Guoin, a French housewife who saw the Indians filing off their gun barrels. There have also been several male claimants to the honor, including a Frenchman named Jacques Duperon Baby, various interpreters, and a disgruntled Ottawa brave known as Mahiganne.

Whether or not Catherine, comely or homely, actually did the deed, her story invariably has a sad but sweet ending. Heartbroken over her unrequited love, years later, as legend has it, she perished during a drunken binge by toppling into a vat of boiling maple syrup.

Be that as it may, Gladwin was well prepared for Pontiac on May 8. The entire garrison stood armed and on the alert when Pontiac and some 300 followers filed into the fort. Variant versions of what happened next also have been perpetuated in the history books. The most stirring has Pontiac and 60 of his braves facing off an equal number of soldiers with drawn swords and leveled muskets. It must have been a good sized room. In any event, as this version alleges, Gladwin then threw open the door to an adjoining hall filled with additional red-coats. Stepping forward and looking Pontiac straight in the eyes, Gladwin pulled one of his brave's blankets aside to reveal his sawed off musket. He then denounced Pontiac and followers as "treacherous cowards."

Pontiac extricated himself from the situation with true

diplomacy. Then the war party made a hasty exit from the fort. Back at his camp, he threw a fit of rage.

Pontiac tried a similar ruse the following day to no avail. Whereupon he gave up any pretext of friendliness by butchering the soldiers and civilians outside the fort, and the siege of Detroit was on.

That siege lasted for 153 days, but the British managed to hold out. Pontiac's failure to take Detroit broke his power, and his followers gradually melted away. Peace was restored until the Revolutionary War again incited red man against white.

Pontiac was tomahawked to death by a Kaskaskia tribesman in 1769 near Cahokia, Illinois.

Charles de Langlade, the Bravest of the Brave

Artist's conception of Charles de Langlade,
who won many a battle but never a war.

Gen. Edward Braddock smiled condescendingly as he listened to Benjamin Franklin's sage advice about Indian warfare. Franklin never forgot his reply: "These savages may indeed be a formidable enemy to the raw American military, but upon the King's regular and disciplined troops, Sir, it is impossible they should make any impression."

Soon after, on June 10, 1775, Braddock led an army of 1,850 from Fort Cumberland, Maryland, to attack the French Fort Duquesne at present-day Pittsburgh. Those "savages" he had held in such contempt cost him his life as well as those of many of his troops in the battle that came to be known as Braddock's Defeat.

It was Charles de Langlade, the Michilimackinac-born "terror of the frontier," who led Michigan and Wisconsin tribesmen to that victory. Furthermore, although Langlade had the misfortune to fight on the losing side in both the French and Indian War and the Revolutionary War, those conflicts might well have turned out differently had Langlade's superiors followed his advice at critical battles.

His father, Sieur Augustine de Langlade, a French nobleman, immigrated to New France and engaged in the Indian trade. By 1720, he had established his headquarters at Fort Michilimackinac, located at present-day Mackinaw City. There, he married Domitilde, sister of a great Ottawa chief, King Nis-so-wa-quet.

Charles, their second child, was born at the Ottawa village adjacent to Fort Michilimackinac in May 1729. Although educated by the Jesuit missionaries there, Langlade seemed destined at an early age for the battlefield.

He participated in his first campaign while but 10 years old. His uncle, King Nis-so-wa-quet, at the urging of the French commandant at Michilimackinac, went on the warpath against the fierce Fox Indians, who were levying excessive tolls on all fur traders who passed their villages on Wisconsin's Fox River. Nis-so-wa-quet had had a dream that revealed he would vanquish his foes should young Langlade accompany the war party. The ensuing battle, during which Langlade and other Indian youths blew on reeds from concealment to confuse the enemy, resulted in a rout of the Fox. Thereafter, whenever the Ottawa took to the warpath, Langlade, whom they named "bravest of the brave," accompanied them.

About 1745, Sieur de Langlade and his son Charles migrated to present-day Green Bay, Wisconsin, where they established a trading post. This was the first permanent settlement in what would become the state of Wisconsin; in fact, Charles Langlade is credited as being "the father of Wisconsin."

In the meantime, George Croghan and other British traders had begun to challenge the French claims to the interior of North American. Croghan, in 1748, erected Fort Pickawillany at present-day Piqua, Ohio. Four years later, under orders from the governor of New France, Marquis Duquesne, Langlade led a band of Ottawa from Michigan who destroyed the fort.

Duquesne next erected a string of forts in Pennsylvania, south of Lake Erie. To counter this French expansion, Virginia Gov. Robert Dinwiddie sent a force under a young surveyor named George Washington to construct a fort at present day Pittsburgh. But the French chased off the construction crew and built Fort Duquesne there. In 1754, Washington's campaign to take the fort resulted in his defeat at Fort Necessity.

In April 1755, Braddock, an imperious commander skilled in European style battle which featured chess-like maneuvers during which armies stood in open ranks and calmly fired at each other, arrived in Virginia to take charge of British forces. Disregarding the advice of colonial militia officers, who knew something about frontier warfare, Braddock led his army of 1,400 British regulars and 450 colonials under command of Washington in a line of march three to four miles long.

26

To accommodate the cumbersome baggage wagons piled high with officers' trunks and fancy mess equipment — some officers even brought their wives on the campaign — engineers had to construct a road ahead of the column. It took Braddock a month to travel only 100 miles.

Langlade's reputation as a frontier fighter and his influence with the Indians prompted Pierre Vaudreuil, who had succeeded Duquesne as governor of New France, to send him to the relief of Fort Duquesne. Langlade assembled some 900 Ottawa, Chippewa, Menominee, Winnebago, Potawatomi, and Huron warriors and Creole voyageurs and quickly made the long journey to Pennsylvania.

As the British slowly drew closer, the French commandant of the fort seemed overwhelmed at the size of the attacking force. But Langlade convinced him to allow his Indians to ambush the British.

Having crossed the Monongahela River below the fort, the British had halted to partake of a formal mid-day meal. Suddenly, from the protective cover of the wooded hillsides along a crescent shaped front, with blood-curdling war whoops, the Indians and French fired volley after volley into the exposed British troops.

The British returned fire, but they could see no targets. They raked the heights with cannon shot but succeeded only in bringing down some branches. British officers, many with napkins still pinned to their breasts, leaped on their mounts and heroically tried to rally the troops. One after another, including Braddock, who took a bullet in the lungs, toppled to the ground.

Periodically, an Indian dashed out to scalp one of the fallen, but that was the only sign of the enemy the British saw. Washington, who had been desperately ill before the battle, performed gallantly. While trying to rally his Virginia militiamen, he had two horses shot out from under him, and three time bullets passed through his hat and clothing. But his bravery had little effect, and the panic-stricken British retreated back across the river. Luckily for

27

the British, the Indians contented themselves with scalping the more than 300 dead and wounded that had been left on the field and pillaging the supply train. Otherwise, the entire force might have been wiped out.

Washington conveyed Braddock out of danger, but the general died four days later. Total British casualties at the Battle of the Wilderness numbered 977 killed or wounded.

The French claimed a glorious victory, but they would not win the war. The British capture of Quebec in 1760, during which Langlade's advice to attack them with Indians while they were exposed was ignored, sealed the fate of New France. Langlade suffered the humiliation of personally surrendering his native Michilimackinac.

Langlade played an important role during Pontiac's Rebellion in 1763, and during the Revolutionary War he again led the northern warriors in savage battle—this time in support of the British.

Following the war, Langlade retired to his home at Green Bay. He remained active until his death in 1800, having fought in 99 battles and skirmishes over his long career. His only regret was that he had not been able to make that record an even 100.

Gnadenhutten, Michigan, and the Scalped Indian Boy

John Heckewelder, Moravian missionary.

Hollywood at its goriest best could not have invented a more horrifying nightmare. The troubled screams of Thomas, a teenage Delaware Indian, had pierced the evening stillness so often over the preceding four years that by 1786, the inhabitants of Gnadenhutten, a tiny Moravian settlement near the present site of Mt. Clemens, had almost grown used to them.

The same grisly dream came to Thomas nightly. A long line of his friends and relatives, Christian Indians, stood bound together, two-by-two. A huge white man slowly advanced along the line calmly bashing in their heads with a cooper's mallet. He grunted each time he struck a blow. He stopped behind Thomas, handed the hammer to another, and said, "That makes 14, my arm fails me, go on in the same way; I think I have done pretty well."

The next thing Thomas knew, he was lying amid a pile of scalped and mutilated bodies. His skull throbbed with an unbearable headache. When he put his hand to the top of his head, he felt a clot of sticky blood in place of hair—he had been scalped!

Then he woke up screaming. His fellow Gnadenhuttenites understood his nightmares. For, what he dreamt had actually happened. Thomas, "the scalped Indian boy," and another Indian youth were the sole survivors of one of the most heinous atrocities in American history, the massacre of 96 unarmed Christian Indians, men, women, and children, at Gnadenhutten, Ohio, on March 8, 1782.

A religious sect that split off from the Greek Orthodox Church in the 9th century, the Moravians practiced pacifism, were zealous missionaries, and decided public issues as well as chose marriage partners by lottery. Under the leadership of Count Zinzindorf, a colony of Moravians emigrated from Germany to America in the early 18th century, establishing their headquarters at Bethlehem, Pennsylvania.

During the 1760's, John Heckewelder launched Moravian missionary activities in the Ohio country. In 1772, he and David Zeisberger founded the first town in Ohio, Shoenbrunn, near present-day New Philadelphia. Four years later, the congregation there numbered 417 people, primarily members of the Delaware Indian tribe. Gnadenhutten, a related mission, lay 10 miles to the south.

In the meantime, the outbreak of the Revolutionary War, during which the Moravians attempted to pursue neutrality, placed them in danger from the Americans, the British, and both sides' Indian allies. In 1776, Heckewelder and Zeisberger abandoned Shoenbrunn and established a new mission to the north, near Sandusky.

In October, 1781, Major Arent Schuyler DePeyster, British commandant at Fort Detroit, summoned Heckewelder and Zeisberger to Detroit to answer charges that the Moravian Indians were aiding the American war effort. While there, they witnessed an Indian war party present American scalps to the British for bounty payments.

The Moravians, however, managed to convince DePeyster of their neutrality, and he allowed them to return to their settlement near Sandusky. But Simon Girty, the "white savage," and other Indian leaders soon prevailed on DePeyster to remand his decision and order all the Moravians and their Indian converts to be rounded up for removal to the vicinity of Detroit where they could be more carefully watched.

In March, 1782, while this forced exodus was in process, a group of Moravian Indians returned to Gnadenhutten to harvest the corn they had left in their fields. They had nearly finished that task when a punitive expedition of Pennsylvania militiamen under Col. David Williamson descended upon them.

Giving the impression that they were friendly, the militiamen convinced the Indians to surrender their arms by promising to lead them eastward to safety. The Pennsylvanians, however, who had suffered bloody raids by Indians loyal to the British, determined to slaughter the Moravian Indians in reprisal. Knowing they were Christian, they allowed them a few hours of prayer before commencing the butchery.

Hit on the head, scalped, and left for dead amid the pile of bodies, Thomas managed to escape to the woods at nightfall and make his way back to Sandusky with news of the massacre. The Gnadenhutten atrocity inspired the western Indians to intensify their bloody forays against the Americans.

Heckewelder, Zeisberger and what was left of their Indian converts sought refuge at Detroit. DePeyster temporarily housed them in the barracks there, and later they lived in residences in the French community. They had ample opportunity to witness everyday life at Detroit which Zeisberger described as "like Sodom, where all sins are committed."

The following summer, a band of Moravians and Indian converts left the Detroit Sodom to found a new town 23 miles to the north on the Huron River. In memory of the tragedy, they also named it Gnadenhutten. There, they soon erected 27 log residences.

Despite many kindnesses shown by DePeyster, Heckewelder considered their four year stay there "that of a cruel exile." They were practically cut off from communication with Detroit, the closest settlement. "In summer," Heckewelder recorded, "the way lay partly through a large swamp covered with tall grass where, besides the probability of being smothered in the mire, the lives of travelers were in imminent danger on account of the incredible number of rattlesnakes, of the most venomous kind; and in winter, the deep snow, the treacherous ice, and the inclement weather made the journey almost impossible."

The densely forested tract where they settled also proved difficult to cultivate. Laboring with axes in summer, the colonists were "tormented by swarms of mosquitoes." Moreover, the native Chippewa did not favor intruders in their ancestral land.

In the spring of 1786, the Moravians abandoned the

Gnadenhutten, Michigan, village and established a settlement in Ohio on the Cayahoga River. There, Thomas, who had developed epilepsy as a result of his scalping, drowned in the river, probably during a seizure. All traces of Gnadenhutten, Michigan, have disappeared.

The River Raisin Massacre

Artist's wood-cut rendition of the River Raisin Massacre on January 23, 1813.

Pvt. Elias Darnell strained his ears above the labored breathing, groans and chattering teeth of the 30 wounded soldiers who lay huddled within the small log house in Frenchtown, now known as Monroe. He listened for the shuffle of moccasins in the snow outside, the creak of the door's leather hinges or the crackle of flames. Throughout that frosty January night in 1813, he repeatedly tossed off the thin blanket beneath which he shivered and went out to check whether the house had been set afire.

Finally, when dawn tinged the eastern horizon, Darnell and his fellow American infantrymen breathed a collective sigh of relief—they had not been massacred by the Indians in the night as they had fully expected. Any time now, the sleighs that had been promised by their British captors would arrive to convey the wounded to safety.

Instead, about an hour after sunrise, a mob of drunken Indians, faces daubed hideous with war paint and brandishing bloodied tomahawks, howled into the settlement.

Following the U.S. declaration of war against Great Britain on June 18, 1812, Darnell had been one of the 2,300 militiamen and regulars who had enlisted from Kentucky. Under command of Gen. James Winchester, a haughty old veteran of the Revolutionary War who little understood the western style of warfare, the four regiments of volunteers marched north to join Gen. William Hull's force at Detroit, then engaged as part of a three pronged invasion of Canada. En route, however, the soldiers learned that Hull had surrendered Detroit without firing a shot.

The Kentucky regiments linked up with the western army under command of Gen. William Henry Harrison, which, as a result of Hull's surrender, was forced to fall back to the Wabash-Maumee river line. That fall, Harrison's men contented themselves with conducting raids against the Indian villages along the Mississinewa River in Indiana and protecting Fort Wayne. By January, however, when the ground had frozen enough to permit travel through the notorious Black Swamp south of Toledo, Harrison's army began an advance towards Detroit.

From his headquarters at Upper Sandusky, Harrison ordered Winchester to move to the Rapids of the Maumee (the present site of Perrysburg, Ohio) and construct sleds in preparation for an attack on Fort Malden, Canada, as soon as the ice on the lake would permit travel. In the meantime, bungling by the army procurement office and private contractors had produced a serious shortage of supplies and munitions. Many of the troops had worn their boots out and now were forced to march through the deep snow with rags wrapped around their feet, ala Valley Forge. Darnell noted in his journal: "Our clothes and blankets looked as if they had never been acquainted with water, but intimately with dirt, smoke, and soot."

During the following week, several of the French inhabitants of Frenchtown on the River Raisin pleaded with Winchester to come to their relief. They reported that a force of approximately 50 Canadian militiamen and 200 Indians was rounding up all American sympathizers there and was preparing to transport a large store of flour and grain from the village to Fort Malden. Against Harrison's orders, Winchester decided to risk an attack on Frenchtown, although even if successful, it would place him in danger of being cut off from his supply base.

On the morning of January 17, approximately 680 soldiers under command of Lt. Col. William Lewis set out from the rapids. They marched along the ice on the shore of Lake Erie and reached the mouth of the River Raisin the following afternoon. The British fired on them with artillery and rifles to no effect as the Kentuckians charged across the river to take the village. The Americans chased the fleeing Canadians and Indians through the woods for two miles, killing and scalping 12 Indians and wounding approximately 50 more.

Three days later, Winchester and 230 additional troops under command of Col. Samuel Wells arrived to reinforce

Frenchtown. Lewis' men had encamped within the palisades of the settlement north of the river. But Wells' regiment pitched their tents in an open, unprotected field to the east of the stockade, a blunder that would cost most of them their lives. Winchester foolishly established his headquarters in the comfortable home of Francis Navarre on the opposite side of the river and over a mile distant from his command.

A Frenchman arrived late that afternoon to report that a large party of British and Indians was en route from Fort Malden to attack, but, according to Darnell, the officers, "who were regaling themselves with whiskey and loaf sugar," refused to believe him.

Within minutes after reveille was beaten at dawn the morning of January 22, the British force under command of Col. Henry Proctor began bombarding the American camp with cannon and mortar. By the time Winchester got to the battlefield, he found Wells' regiment in the unprotected field being cut to pieces by the British artillery. He ordered them to retreat and reform at the river bank, but in the confusion, the retreat turned into a disorderly rout. Practically all of Wells' men were killed, wounded, or captured. Winchester himself also fell into enemy hands.

The 400 or 500 Kentuckians within the stockade fared better, although they only had about 10 rounds of ammunition each. Firing through portholes in the pickets, they repulsed several British attacks with little loss on their own part. Finally, the British ceased fire and pulled back.

Loaves of bread were passed out to the American defenders, and, as Darnell and the others "sat composedly eating and watching the enemy at the same time," they discovered a white flag approaching. To their amazement and disgust, they learned that Winchester had surrendered them. The ranking American officer, a Major Madison, refused to comply until Proctor gave his assurances that the wounded would be protected against the Indians. Then the Kentuckians marched out and "in the heat and bitterness of spirit," grounded their arms.

Fearful of a counterattack by the remainder of Harrison's army, the British marched those prisoners able to travel to Fort Malden. Approximately 80 wounded Americans were left without guards with the promise that the sleighs would be sent the next morning for them. Darnell, whose brother was severely injured, volunteered to remain with the wounded.

The mob of drunken Indians who returned to Frenchtown the following morning "rushed on the wounded, and, in their barbarous manner, shot, and tomahawked, and scalped them; and cruelly mangled their naked bodies while they lay agonizing and weltering in their blood." They set fire to the homes that housed the wounded and, when the screaming Americans within tried to escape out the windows, clubbed them back into the flames. The Indians murdered some 60-80 wounded Americans during the atrocity that came to be known as the River Raisin Massacre.

The Indians marched Darnell and a few of the others able to travel to various Indian villages where they were adopted into the tribe in place of braves who had died during the battle. He eventually escaped and made his way back to Kentucky, where he published the journal of his harrowing experiences.

"Remember the Raisin" became the battle cry of Harrison's western army, which decisively defeated Proctor's force at the Battle of the Thames, Canada, on October 5, 1813.

By Horned Breeze and Paddle Wheels: The Walk-in-the-Water

The Walk-in-the-Water chugging up the Detroit River.

The great smokestack that jutted up between the masts of the Walk-in-the-Water belched a thick, black stream of soot and flickering sparks. Its two paddle wheels churned the water white. The Indians who pointed and yelled from the Canadian side of the Detroit River had heard rumors that the Great White Father was sending a big canoe drawn by a sturgeon, but they little expected such a monster.

As if that were not enough commotion, a cannon on the bow of the steamship boomed out a welcome. At that sound, most of Detroit's population dropped what they were doing to rush to the newly constructed wharf at the foot of Bates Street. Conspicuous among the several hundred people who awaited the arrival of this first steamboat to ply the water of lakes Erie, Huron, and Michigan was Uncle Ben Woodworth, proud proprietor of the newly named Steamboat Hotel.

It was the morning of August 27, 1818, a milestone in the history of Detroit. No longer would the frontier settlement be isolated by the vagaries of sailing vessels.

Eleven years before, Robert Fulton's Clermont had splashed up the Hudson River to demonstrate the feasibility of the steamship. A Canadian steamer, the Frontenac, and a similar American vessel, the Ontario, had been launched on Lake Ontario in 1817. The following year, a group of wealthy New York City investors determined to place an experimental steamship on Lake Erie.

Black Rock, a settlement on the Niagara River at the mouth of Scajaguada Creek, which then rivaled nearby Buffalo as a port, was selected as the shipyard. Noah Brown laid the keel of the vessel early in the spring of 1818, and the hull was launched on May 28.

The ship was a cross between Fulton's Clermont and a clipper ship. High in the stern and the bow, the vessel was about 140 feet long and 32 feet wide with a displacement of 330 tons. Its masts were equipped with sails to supplement the two paddle wheels located midship. A boiler 20

40

feet long by 9 feet in diameter lay forward of the paddle wheels. Named the Walk-in-the-Water in honor of a local Wyandotte chief of some distinction, she was fully completed in mid-August.

On August 23, Capt. Job Fish bawled out the order to cast off through a "speaking trumpet", and the Walk-in-the-Water began its maiden voyage up the Niagara River. Unfortunately, its paddles proved unable to make much headway against the swift current. Capt. Fish was forced to resort to a "horned breeze" in the form of 16 yoke of oxen that pulled the vessel along from shore.

Twenty-nine brave passengers had boarded the steamer. Among them were the Earl of Selkirk and his countess en route to establish a colony in Ontario; Lt. Col. Henry Leavenworth, whose name is honored by a Kansas city and fort; and Maj. Abraham Edwards, who would later run the federal land office located in the settlement of Kalamazoo.

Once out on Lake Erie, the steamer clipped along at a fairly good pace. Leaving Buffalo at 1:30 p.m., five hours later she reached Dunkirk. All the while, her fireman fed the furnace with great quantities of well-seasoned pine, hemlock, and basswood. Capt. Fish slowed the ship down during the night so as not to bypass Erie, where he landed to take on another supply of cord wood the next morning. From there, she steamed to Cleveland, Sandusky, and Venice, where again the wood was replenished.

Arriving at the mouth of the Detroit River on the evening of the 26th, Fish anchored the Walk-in-the-Water overnight. The next morning, a contingent of prominent Detroit citizens rowed down the river to board her for the gala docking ceremonies. It was about 10:00 a.m. when that momentous event occurred. Much to the captain's embarrassment, however, his landing proved nearly disastrous.

He barked crisp orders through the gleaming speaking trumpet, but the clumsy craft would not respond. After sliding past the wharf and backing up several times, finally the Walk-in-the-Water crashed into the dock with a force that nearly toppled the waiting crowd into the drink—luckily, the pilings held. The entire voyage had taken 44 hours and 10 minutes.

"The passage between this place and Buffalo," wrote the editor of the *Detroit Gazette* in the next day's issue, "is now, not merely tolerable, but truly pleasant." The Walk-in-the-Water soon established a regular biweekly schedule between Black Rock and Detroit. The initial cabin fare of $18.00 was later reduced to $12.00.

In 1819, the Walk-in-the-Water made a run from Detroit to Mackinac Island, thus becoming the first steamship on Lake Huron. Two years later, she ventured out into Lake Michigan, carrying 200 passengers to Green Bay.

For three years, the steamer faithfully carried thousands of passengers without mishap. Then, on October 21, 1821, the "horned breeze" pulled her up the Niagara River for her last voyage. Scarcely out of port, she encountered a vicious gale. Capt. Jedediah Rogers, who had replaced Fish, turned her about in an attempt to return to the shelter of Black Rock.

Unable to find his way in the dark and fearful of running aground, Rogers anchored offshore from Buffalo. But the vessel began to take on so much water that Rogers cut the anchor rope in hopes of drifting ashore. Fortunately, the great waves swept her onto the beach, a sailor made it through the surf with a line, and everyone aboard was rescued.

The hull of the Walk-in-the-Water was a total loss, but the engine and boiler were salvaged and installed in the second steamship on Lake Erie, the Superior.

By 1825, when the opening of the Erie Canal ushered in a wave of immigration to Michigan Territory, the Henry Clay had also joined the Superior in providing transportation service to Detroit.

When the Superior was converted to a sailing vessel in 1835, the original engine that powered the Walk-in-the-Water was installed in the Charles Townsend. After many years of service, it was removed and used as late as 1902 in a Buffalo machine shop.

Mind Your Manners and Pass the Bear

Gurdon Hubbard, decades after his bear meat feast.

G urdon S. Hubbard stared in disbelief at the big wooden bowl heaped high with steaming chunks of fat bear meat. A similar bowl sat before each of the Indians and American Fur Company traders who sat cross-legged around the interior of the smoked-filled lodge. Hubbard's helping, however, was clearly the largest—more meat than three men could eat with comfort. Then an Ottawa squaw solemnly skimmed a generous helping of the syrupy bear grease which had risen to the top of the cooking pot and ladled it over Hubbard's meat.

Fellow fur trader, Jacques Dufrain, had already briefed Hubbard on the propriety of the occasion. Everyone present must eat all that was placed before him--failure to do so would be considered an unpardonable insult to the Indians and an offense to the Great Spirit.

Astonished at the size of his helping, Hubbard whispered to Dufrain, "They have given me more than the others, and it is impossible for me to swallow it all."

Dufrain responded: "They have given you the best portion as a compliment; you must receive it, and eat and drink every bit and every drop, otherwise we shall have trouble. I am sorry for you, as well as for myself, and wish it had been a cub instead of a fat bear, but I shall eat mine if it kills me."

It was January 1820. Seventeen-year-old Hubbard, Dufrain, and a voyageur had traveled from their winter headquarters on Muskegon Lake some 50 miles into the snow covered wilderness to the Ottawa village to trade furs. Unused to traveling on snowshoes while carrying a 50 pound pack, Hubbard's feet had become bruised and swollen, a complaint known by the voyageurs as "mal du raquette." Nevertheless, the tenderfoot limped along for three days, recuperating at an Indian camp where they stopped for several days to trade furs.

From there, they pushed on for two more days to another Ottawa village. Overjoyed to see their white visitors, the Indians prepared a grand bear meat feast in their honor. The ceremony began about 8 that evening. After speeches and a prayer to the Great Spirit to "favor them in the chase and keep them well and free from harm," the culinary orgy began.

Seated in a dark corner of the birch-bark lodge, Hubbard had not taken many bites of the greasy meat before he realized his case was hopeless. Fortunately, he was wearing a French-style garment with a hood into which he cautiously slipped most of the meat. But the grease soaked through his shirt, and when he felt it trickling down his back, he began to squirm.

Explaining to Dufrain in Ottawa that he needed to get a breath of air, Hubbard also asked him not to let his bowl get tipped over while he was gone. While the Indians roared with laughter, he made a hasty exit, quickly unloaded his hood to a pack of dogs, returned, and somehow managed to quaff down the remainder of the oily broth.

Hubbard's close encounter with the perils of Indian etiquette was but one of many Michigan adventures he recorded in a diary published by his wife two years after he died in 1886. *The Autobiography of Gurdon Saltonstall Hubbard* remains a classic account of the glory days of the Mackinac Island fur-trading empire.

Born in Windsor, Vermont, in 1802, Hubbard moved with his family to Montreal in 1815. At the age of 16, he secured a job as a clerk with John Jacob Astor's American Fur Co. at a wage of $120 per year. Embarking from Montreal on May 13, 1818, in a fleet of bateaux heavily laden with trade goods and rowed by steel-sinewed voyageurs, Hubbard made the arduous seven-week journey to Mackinac Island.

Following a summer of hard work sorting and pressing into bales the thousands of pelts which flowed there via a fur-trading network that stretched from the Lake of the Woods to the Missouri River, Hubbard's first trading assignment was in the Illinois country the following winter.

The next season, he set out with veteran trader Dufrain and two voyageurs to work among the Ottawa who dwelt during the winter in small bands along the Muskegon River, a choice trapping region. Held up by several storms en route, they arrived at the mouth of the Muskegon River on December 10, 1819, to find Muskegon Lake already frozen over.

Dropping their plans to establish headquarters further upstream, the men chopped their way through the ice to an abandoned post on the shore of Muskegon Lake. Hubbard remained there while the other three traders carried packs of trade goods into the interior in search of Indian camps. He lived in solitude for an entire month, subsisting on a store of dried corn, small game, and fish he speared through the ice.

When his companions returned to replenish their trade goods, Hubbard, thoroughly bored with his solitary existence, left one of the voyageurs to guard the post and took his place on the fur-trading trail. Mal du raquette and the bear meat feast were but two of the many adventures which forever etched that winter in his memory. Hubbard succeeded in amassing a choice load of furs, but tragically, Dufrain, weakened because of exposure while lost in the woods, died.

During the 15 years he plied the life of a fur trader, Hubbard's prowess in walking as many as 60 miles a day won him the title Pa-pa-ma-ta-be, "The Swift Walker." Other remarkable experiences he recorded in his autobiography include spending the winter of 1820-21 at a trading post located near the present intersection of Kalamazoo's Paterson Street and Riverview Drive, a visit to the ancient wooden cross that marked Father Marquette's grave at Ludington, and the witnessing of the accidental shooting of Alexis St. Martin, "the man with the window in his stomach."

Although he had to eat it now and then, Hubbard never cared too much for bear meat following his Indian feast in 1820. Pork was more to his liking, and in 1834, he settled in Chicago where, ironically, he became the "largest meat packer in the West."

Grand Island, Ojibwa Eden

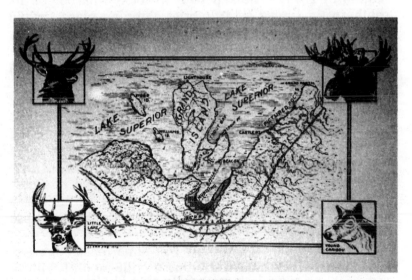

*Promotional map of Grand Island issued by the
Cleveland Cliffs Iron Co., ca. 1904.*

G itchee Manitou, the Great Spirit, was not pleased with his handiwork. The giant creatures he had created were too big—far too big. Should he breathe life into them, they might become more powerful than himself. So he cast them away.

Over the eons, their gigantic bodies, Ojibwa traditions decreed, were petrified into the hills that surround Munising on the southern shore of Lake Superior. Another of those sleeping giants formed eight-mile-long Grand Island, a pristine oasis of natural beauty crouched off the coast of Munising. The two smaller islands to the west are the great creature's hands.

The largest island on Lake Superior's southern shore, long a dwelling place of the native Ojibwa and before them the unknown tribes they supplanted, Grand Island appeared on the first map of Lake Superior made by the Jesuit fathers in 1671. The superb land-locked harbor on its southern tip served as a favorite camping place for the hardy voyageurs who paddled their great birch-bark canoes in the quest of furs. But, apart from a few scattered references by the early explorers, the island remained shrouded in mystery until 1820.

On June 21 of that year, a team of explorers headed by Territorial Gov. Lewis Cass beached their bateaux on the sandy shore of Grand Island's Murray Bay. The island tribesmen greeted their white visitors with open arms and a peace pipe. That evening, they regaled the expedition members with a ceremonial dance, songs, and orations. The account of the expedition published by its mineralogist, Henry Rowe Schoolcraft, offers an intimate glimpse into Ojibwa culture.

Schoolcraft, who would later win fame for his pioneering ethnological studies including a collection of Ojibwa lodge tales that inspired Henry Wadsworth Longfellow to write the Song of Hiawatha, was particularly impressed with a "tall and beautiful youth, with a manly countenance, expressive eyes, and formed with the most perfect symmetry." The young Indian, Schoolcraft learned, was the sole survivor of a recent battle with the tribe's ancient enemies, the Sioux, who dwelt to the west.

The story of that adventure, as recorded by Schoolcraft, might well have formed the theme of a Greek tragedy:

The Grand Island band, it seems, had been chided by the neighboring Ojibwa for their failure to take an active role in the longstanding war with the Sioux. To redeem their honor, 13 young warriors decided to conduct a daring foray. They managed to travel undetected into the midst of enemy territory, when suddenly they stumbled upon a war party 10 times their own number.

Since peace negotiations between the tribes had begun, the Sioux were willing to let them return home. But the Ojibwa warriors replied "that they had come a great way to meet them, that they wanted to test their courage, and that they rejoiced there was now an opportunity presented."

That evening, the Ojibwa readied themselves for a fight to the death. They dug two large intrenchments, in preparation for their last stand, where they intended "to sell their lives at the dearest rate."

The following morning, they attacked the Sioux encampment but were soon driven back to their fortifications. There, they continued to fight, pouring a deadly fire into the attacking force and bringing down twice their own number. Finally, they ran out of ammunition, and the Sioux rushed the fortification, tomahawking every one of them—every one but the youth, that is, who had been stationed on a nearby hilltop to carry the story of their bravery back to the tribe.

Making his way back to Grand Island, "he sang the exploits of his departed friends" who had redeemed their honor at the cost of their lives. Other "kamikaze" exploits run as a common thread through Ojibwa tradition. There was the ancient Grand Island hornet rite, for example. Naked young braves would arm themselves with a short stick and sally forth to attack a hornet's nest. Whoever

49

stood his ground the longest while being repeatedly stung by the angry insects was judged the bravest.

Little wonder that, by the time Schoolcraft returned to the island in 1832, the total number of adult men had dropped to seven. It was at that point that the Grand Island tribe faced a threat to their existence even more foreboding than their own suicidal tendencies in the form of zealous Methodist missionaries.

George Copway, a young Ojibwa chief who had been converted to the Methodist faith, stopped at the island while en route to Sault Ste. Marie in 1835. He noticed that one of the sandy points on the southern tip of the island had disappeared. A local trader, Charles Holiday, told him that the Indians believed "the Great Spirit had removed from under that point to some other point, because the Methodist missionaries had encamped there the previous fall, and had, by their prayers, driven the Spirit from under the point." The Indians did not want the missionaries to camp on their island anymore, fearing the whole island would sink.

That wish notwithstanding, all but 640 of Grand Island's 13,500 acres were signed away by certain Ojibwa chiefs as a condition of the 1836 Treaty of Washington. Four years later, Abraham Williams and family arrived from Vermont to become the island's first permanent white residents.

The little settlement they constructed on the southern tip of the island, known as Williams Landing, thrived until the up-and-coming town of Munising on the mainland eclipsed it in the 1870's.

In 1900, the Cleveland-Cliffs Iron Co. acquired the entire island for approximately $93,000. Company President William G. Mather preserved the northern Eden as a private game preserve. He imported elk, albino deer, caribou, and grouse and planted trout and bass in the island's lakes and streams.

Williams' house was restored and converted into a hotel. It and an adjoining inn constructed in 1909 accommodated

50

150 guests. The Cleveland-Cliffs' Grand Island Park became a fashionable resort for well-heeled nature enthusiasts. The company continued to operate the resort until 1958.

The Trust for Public Land bought the island from Cleveland-Cliffs in 1988. Plans are currently underway for acquisition by the U.S. Forest Service and the creation of a national recreation area.

Drummond Island's Brief Era of Glory

Dr. John Bigsby's 1823 sketch of Fort Drummond on Drummond Island.

John Bigsby remembered for decades that scene of dazzling beauty. It was a summer day in 1823 when the big birch-bark canoe he sat in neared Whitney Bay at the southeastern tip of Drummond Island. Suddenly, the sun burst through the morning fog. Across the sparkling azure water, he saw a "forest of wigwams" ranked along the beach and the whitewashed buildings of Fort Drummond dotting the heights beyond.

The Ottawa who had transported him from Mackinac Island had landed at a point three miles back to don ceremonial finery and paint their faces with gaudy designs. Now, as the fleet of 25 canoes skimmed over the tranquil waters of the bay, the Ottawa men aboard arose in majestic splendor to better display their colorful costumes.

They wore red shirts of stiffened calico and chamois leather leggings embroidered with porcupine quills and fringed with red moose-hair. Breastplates and armlets of silver gleamed in the sun. Some sported European-style hats with silver bands and ostrich feathers, others high, round caps covered with red moose-hair that streamed back in the breeze. Festooned with blue and white beads, the women paddlers also wore numerous silver anklets and armlets.

The Union Jack flapped from the sterns of two of the canoes carrying chiefs. Red pennants flew from the the others. The crowd of British soldiers, traders, and fellow tribesmen assembled on the beach burst into a spontaneous cheer in admiration of the rare spectacle.

It was the heyday of the northern fur trade as well as of the island that served as the British counterpart to Mackinac Island. Yet, few among those gathered on Drummond Island that day had not seen the the handwriting on the wall.

Following the Revolutionary War, in 1796, the British had relinquished Mackinac Island to the Americans and established another fort on St. Joseph Island in the St. Marys River. But the British recaptured Mackinac Island during the War of 1812. However, the Treaty of Ghent, which ended that war, called for a "status quo ante bellum", and the British again withdrew from the island in 1815.

Since the fort on St. Joseph Island had been razed by the Americans during the war, nearby Drummond Island was selected as the next site for the army garrison stationed to protect British fur-trading interests in the upper Great Lakes. Both the island and the fort built at its southeastern tip were named in honor of Gen. Sir Gordon Drummond, commander of the British forces in Canada.

Although Col. Robert McDouall, commander of the British garrison, recognized that Drummond Island was a less strategic location than Mackinac, he fully intended to render the new fort the "Gilbraltar of the West." One nagging factor, however, stood in his way. Since the joint boundary commission had yet to run its survey to determine the actual Canadian/U.S. border, Drummond Island might belong to the U.S. The cost-conscious British home government dispatched an order forbidding the construction of fortifications pending the report of the boundary commissioners.

Nevertheless, shelter against the harsh northern climate was essential. During the next few years, the British erected wooden barracks, a block house, a hospital, storehouses, etc. Eventually, some 200 structures, including the civilian residences and trader's huts at the adjacent village platted out as Fort Collier, took shape.

The main object of the British presence was to retain the loyalty of the Indians against American encroachments in the fur trade. Although the garrison itself was poorly supplied, the British continued to distribute generous annual presents to the Indians. Each summer, as many as 4,500 Ottawa, Chippewa, and Potawatomi journeyed to Drummond Island to receive presents and to trade furs. The Indians also knew how to play the nations against each other, and while in the vicinity, they collected similar gifts from the Americans at Mackinac Island.

Finally, in 1822, the boundary commission delivered its report. St. Joseph Island was awarded to the British, but Drummond Island was American soil. Bigsby, who had served as medical officer and secretary to the British Boundary Commission, tarried another year in the north country to study its geology and insects.

He found the post at Drummond Island "healthy, but most dismal—a mere heap of rocks on the edge of an impenetrable medley of morass, ponds, and matted woods." The two companies of infantry stationed there led a boring life, with little to do "save read, hunt for fossils, fish, shoot, cut down trees, and plant potatoes," the only crop that would grow. Against strict orders, they imbibed whiskey at the village, and drunkenness posed a constant problem. Desertion, understandably, also proved a common occurrence.

Bigsby learned of a tragic event that had taken place the previous year. Five men had deserted in an attempt to gain sanctuary on Mackinac Island. The British commander posted a reward for their capture. A half-dozen Indians set out in pursuit, took a shortcut, and set up an ambush. They returned a few days later with the AWOL soldiers' heads in a bag. It was not long before an order arrived from headquarters in Quebec that forbade the "employment of Indians in capturing deserters."

Bigsby remained a fortnight on Drummond Island, then paid a visit to Mackinac Island, approximately 35 miles to the west. Following a short stay there, he secured a ride back to Drummond Island with Chief Blackbird of the Harbor Springs area, who, with 700 of his people, was on his way to receive the annual presents from the British government.

That voyage also proved memorable for Bigsby. He squeezed into a large canoe already loaded down with the chief, four braves, four squaws, six children, two or three dogs, and a half-tamed young black bear. The braves enjoyed the ride, smoking all the while, as the women did all the rowing. But whatever discomfort Bigsby experienced was amply compensated for by the breathtaking scenery en route, especially the picturesque arrival ceremony.

Bigsby eventually booked passage on a sloop bound for Detroit. He returned to England, where in 1850, he published his travel adventures under the noteworthy title, *The Shoe and the Canoe*.

The British hastily abandoned Drummond Island in 1828, leaving a deserted village replete with furnishings and supplies and a well- filled cemetery, the final resting place for those who had died during the 13-year occupation of the island.

What became of the remains of the five deserters who paid a capital punishment for their crimes remains a mystery. However, modern-day visitors to Drummond Island are still regaled by the legend of the ghostly Redcoats that wander the islands at night in quest of their missing heads.

The Erie Canal, Immigrant Highway to Michigania

With the canal aqueduct over the Mohawk River in the background, this 1825 lithograph portrays the gala opening ceremonies of the Erie Canal.

C linton's Big Ditch," his political enemies howled, was the folly of the ages. But while they scoffed, the Erie Canal, long championed by New York Gov. DeWitt Clinton, inched its way across the state. When it finally opened in 1825, a 363-mile ribbon of water linked the Hudson River with Lake Erie.

Completed at a cost of $7.6 million in an era when construction laborers considered themselves fortunate to earn 75 cents for a dawn-to-dusk workday, the Erie Canal was soon proclaimed the engineering marvel of its age. It, more than any other factor, would earn New York the title of Empire State and firmly crown New York City as America's commercial capital.

The Erie Canal's impact on Michigan Territory was scarcely less dramatic. Difficulty of access, coupled with bad publicity which branded the region a morass unfit for habitation, had caused the territory to be largely by-passed by the tide of westward immigration. But the relatively cheap and easy transportation afforded by the canal lured a growing swell of land-lookers into Michigan. Their reports soon dispelled the adverse myths about its terrain. In the ensuring decade, the canal carried hordes of immigrants and land speculators to Michigan's lush wilderness as well as the peninsula's bountiful harvest of furs, wood products, grain, and other commodities to eastern markets.

Detroit, a sleepy little French village in 1825, soon blossomed into a bustling staging ground for Michigan pioneers. Many came from New England to seek their fortune on the Michigan frontier. Many more, the sons and daughters of those who had pioneered western New York the generation before, set their sights on Michigania, whose lakes, streams, and oak openings reminded them of home. Soon New York place names such as Utica, Rochester, Livonia, Albion, New Buffalo, and, appropriately, DeWitt and Clinton dotted the Michigan map. The census of 1850 revealed that nearly one third of Michigan's population had been born in New York state.

A water highway that would link New York's fortunes with the western Great Lakes region had been suggested by several visionaries during the decades that preceded the War of 1812. But it was the canal's most stalwart advocate, Gov. DeWitt Clinton, who took the bull by the horns and got the project started on July 4, 1817.

Using primitive construction techniques, which relied heavily on the sweat of ditch diggers, primarily Irish, the middle section of the canal, a 94-mile stretch from Utica to Montezuma had been scoured out by the summer of 1820. Originally, the canal was 4 feet deep and 40 feet wide at the surface, sloping to 20 feet wide at the bottom.

Then, contractors tackled simultaneously the more difficult end sections of the project. Much of its course had to be chiseled out of bedrock. A total of 84 lift locks were required to carry the canal nearly 700 vertical feet over rocky obstacles. Aqueducts bridged fast flowing streams. One of the most spectacular carried the canal across the Mohawk River on a bridge 1,188 feet long.

Finally, in October 1825, Clinton led a grand aquatic procession from Albany to New York Harbor, where he triumphantly poured a keg of Lake Erie water into the Atlantic Ocean.

Assisted by a burgeoning fleet of Lake Erie steamers carrying freight and passengers from Buffalo to Detroit, the great rush for the Michigan bonanza was on.

A popular immigrant song of the era celebrated the canal's significance:

"Then there's the State of New York, where some are very rich;
Themselves and a few others have dug a mighty ditch,
To render it more easy for us to find the way,
A sail upon the waters to Michigania--
Yea, yea, yea, to Michigania."

Despite the relative ease of travel on the Erie Canal, the journey westward was still no picnic. The long narrow, snub-nosed packet boats were propelled by slow-moving horse, mule or ox teams that plodded along canal paths bordering the stream. Traveling day and night with the exception of Sunday, it took Baptist missionary Leonard Slater nine days to make a trip on the canal from Albany to Buffalo in 1826. Another two days on Lake Erie landed him in Detroit.

While far less hazardous than the other available means of transportation, travel on the Erie Canal, however, was not without its dangers. More than one unwary passenger, for example, was knocked overboard while the boat passed under one of the many low bridges along the route.

Elisha Loomis, of Rochester, New York, traveled on the canal to Buffalo and hence to Michigan in 1830. He noted that some bridges were so low that everyone had to go below deck to avoid being crushed while at others everyone on deck needed merely press themselves flat.

Loomis recalled an amusing incident which occurred on a canal trip he had made in 1828, during the presidential campaign that pitted Andrew Jackson against John Quincy Adams. As the boat approached a bridge, someone called out, "All those that are for Jackson will go down upon their knees." The entire party, out of necessity, had to thus cast their vote for Jackson. The Democratic triumph was short lived, however. As the boat emerged from under the bridge, a Republican advocate cried out, "Let those that are for Adams rise up."

Traffic on the canal grew at a phenomenal rate. Not only did a major portion of the immigrants who swelled Michigan's population six fold during the decade of the 1830's travel westward on the canal, but the volume of freight flowing eastward increased proportionally. In 1826, 7,000 boat loads of western products arrived at Albany. Ten years later, 3,000 boats plied the length of the canal, and that number grew to 5,000 by 1850.

Meanwhile, steps had been taken to enlarge the canal. In 1836, construction projects to widen and deepen the canal commenced. By 1862, the entire Erie Canal had been enlarged. Between 1903 and 1918, the much larger Barge Canal replaced the old Erie Canal.

Remembering Waukazoo

Waukazoo as depicted in Flavius Littlejohn's "Legends of Michigan..."
published in Allegan in 1875

Pontiac, Pokagon and Petoskey—their names live on across the Michigan map. Potawatomi, Ottawa, Huron, and Ojibwa chiefs: Okemos and Owosso, Missaukee and Mecosta, White Pigeon and Waiska, Noonday, Shavehead, Pewamo, Tecumseh, and Keewahdin—where once they ruled wilderness domains, cities, counties, roads and lakes mark their passing.

Some made the peninsulas ring with war whoops. Implacable enemies to the end, their very names conjure up tomahawks and scalping knives, ambush and torture, flaming arrows in the night.

Many others offered the hand of friendship. They schooled the white man in the ways of the woods, helped hoist heavy logs at frontier raisings and padded silently into hungry settlements bearing haunches of venison and mococks of maple sugar. But when the starving times ended and fields of grain waved over ancestral hunting grounds, they too walked the trail of tears until only scattered remnants huddled in poverty, prey to trader's rum and Yankee greed.

Whether site-namers remembered the red man's generosity or simply admired the rhythmic roll of aboriginal words is open to conjecture. But one thing is certain. Behind each of the place names commemorating Indian chiefs which dot our state lies a story—a story worth remembering.

Take, for example, Waukazoo, an affluent resort suburb on the north shore of Holland's Lake Macatawa. Only by delving into rare books, faded manuscripts and dimly remembered legends can light be shed on Waukazoo, the man.

Chief Andrew Blackbird, an educated Ottawa from Harbor Springs, told of the early life of Waukazoo in his *History of the Ottawa and Chippewa Indians,* published in 1887. Known as a great prophet and magician, Joseph Waukazoo or Agemah, along with his brother, Blackbird's father, spent 20 years of his early manhood hunting and trapping in Manitoba.

Blackbird's father remembered with bitterness the treat-

62

ment they had received from the British fur traders: "liquor sold to the Indians measured with a woman's thimble, a thimbleful for one dollar; one wooden coarse comb for two beaver skins; a double handful of salt for one beaver skin--and so on, in proportion to everything else, the poor Indian had to give pile upon pile of beaver skins, which might be worth two or three hundred dollars, for a few yards of flimsy cloth." Worse yet, the white traders routinely took Indian wives, leaving them and the children they had bore to shift for themselves when they rejoined their legally married spouses back East.

By around 1800, the brothers had evidently had enough of such maltreatment. They tried their fortunes across the border at the major Ottawa concentration in the Little Traverse Bay area. The Ottawa, whose territory encompassed the region from the Straits south to the Kalamazoo River Valley, practiced a migratory existence, spending the warm months to the north and the cold seasons at villages along streams to the south.

By the first decade of the 19th century, Waukazoo had, according to Flavius Littlejohn, emerged as the dominant Ottawa chief in southern Michigan with his village located at the present site of Saugatuck. Littlejohn, who settled in Allegan in 1836 and carved out a notable career as an itinerant circuit court judge, spent the succeeding four decades collecting Indian oral traditions which he published in 1875 as *Legends of Michigan and the Old North West*. He described Waukazoo, a leading character in his book, as "widely known and justly celebrated for his sagacity in matters of home policy, as well as for his shrewd, far-reaching diplomatic views in his intercourse with adjacent tribes."

But Waukazoo's shrewdness and diplomacy proved powerless against the hordes of white settlers who streamed into southwestern Michigan in the 1830's. Their villages soon dotted the length of the Kalamazoo River. Waukazoo, apparently, saw the handwriting on the wall, accepting the only hope for his people's survival as cooperation with the whites and acculturation to their ways.

In late fall 1837, Waukazoo led a delegation from his northern village in Emmet County in search of a Protestant missionary. At a powwow held in Allegan, Waukazoo delivered an impassioned oration which so moved the Rev. George Nelson Smith, a young Congregationalist minister who had previously founded churches in Richland, Otsego and Plainwell, that he determined to devote his life to missionary work among the Indians.

The following year, a group of influential Allegan County pioneers formed the "Western Society to Benefit the Indians" and named Smith their general agent. In December 1838, he established a temporary colony site at Allegan with 30 Indian families, including Waukazoo's, participating. Smith and his wife Arvilla soon opened a school where they taught the "three r's" and the rudiments of the white man's agricultural and domestic skills.

By the spring of 1839, the Allegan colony had swelled to 300 Indian families. It clearly needed a permanent, more isolated location. Following an intensive search, Waukazoo, Smith and the other tribal leaders purchased a site for the Indian village near the present location of downtown Holland.

Smith's mission, which he named Old Wing in honor of a recently deceased chief, was located six miles to the east in Allegan County's Fillmore Township. Despite the privations suffered by the Smiths during the initial period and internal discord arising from visits by Father Andreas Viszosky, a priest from Grand Rapids who also established a mission at Waukazoo's village, the colony prospered.

On October 18, 1845, Waukazoo "died happy," comforted, no doubt, by the white man's religion he had accepted and in the belief that his people had found a secure home. Smith preached at the funeral and then recorded in his diary: "Chief's coffin was put by the side of his mother's so that they both made one grave. Perhaps in that grave is

64

buried the hope of our Mission..."

Alas, Smith's diary entry proved prophetic. The present site of Holland was far too alluring to be left in the hands of Waukazoo's band. In 1847, the Rev. Albertus VanRaalte led an exodus of Dutch immigrants to an Ottawa County Zion.

Unfamiliar with the red man's ethics, the Hollanders appropriated Indian corn fields in their owner's absence, carried home as a providential blessing venison found hanging in the woods, burned caches of sap troughs for kindling and polluted wells.

In 1849, Smith left with the last of the Waukazoo band for a new home in the Leelanau Peninsula. They named that colony Waukazooville, after Peter Waukazoo, who had succeeded his father as chief. Five years later came the beginnings of the adjacent white settlement of Northport, which soon swallowed up the Indian village, and Waukazooville, too, became only a memory.

Waukazoo made the map again, however, when turn-of-the-century real estate promoters thought it a pleasing appellation for a fancy resort community on the north shore of Lake Macatawa.

Now, nearly a century and a half after the demise of the old chief who once held sway over a wilderness empire, nattily dressed Dutch descendants steer expensive cars down Waukazoo Drive and pedal bicycles along the Waukazoo Trail.

Honest John Ball,
Landlooker

John Ball shown holding his daughter, Mary Joanna, in 1867.

John Ball gazed in awe at the forest giant. A white oak, its seven-foot-thick trunk rose to a height of 70 feet before the first of its great boughs thrust out to form a rust-colored canopy of leaves. It was the largest tree he had ever seen in Michigan.

White oaks had value, particularly for ship-building purposes, and the ultimate fate of that tree was to be cross-cut into logs and sent east for naval use. But such hardwood prizes were actually of secondary concern. The primary goal of Ball, one of the vanguard of an army of landlookers and timber cruisers who tramped the Michigan wilderness, was to locate stands of white pine—soft, straight-grained, and light—the preferred building lumber of the time.

Ball, in company with a Mr. Anderson, had left Ionia, the site of the Federal land office for the Grand River Valley, early in the morning of November 3, 1836, on a timber-prospecting foray. Their first day's ride brought them to the frontier outpost of Grand Rapids, where they spent the night at the Eagle Tavern.

Back in the saddle at dawn, they arrived in Grandville mid-morning, hoping to obtain breakfast. That community, however, had not matured to the extent of boasting a tavern. So a settler there promised to keep their horses during their trek into the woods, and his wife managed to scrape together a meager breakfast. But so poorly provisioned were they and their other Grandville neighbors that they could not spare the supplies the travelers tried to buy for their wilderness sustenance.

Eventually, Ball and Anderson succeeded in coaxing some raw beef and an unleavened loaf of bread from a woman who was boarding a gang of sawmill construction workers on Rush Creek. Thusly armed with what amounted to enough food for one meal, the landlookers boldly struck out due west into the untracked forest.

By nightfall, they had reached what is now southern Blendon Township in Ottawa County. They pitched camp on a small creek which meandered through a beech and

67

maple forest. Having built a campfire and cooked and ate their steaks, the two wrapped themselves up in their blankets and "slept as well as the tramping deer and howling wolves" would allow.

The following day's explorations yielded but one small tract of pine. Out of food and hungry, the men decided to retreat out of the woods before nightfall. Taking a route more to the north, however, they stumbled upon a dense forest of virgin white pine. Excitedly, they began following its course to the west to determine the extent of their discovery. Nightfall overtook them, and they again wrapped themselves up and turned in. The next morning, they found themselves covered with a blanket of snow.

Still, they spent most of the next day exploring the pine lands, until, growing weak from hunger, they realized they had to leave their find or perish. They stumbled back to Grandville, having spent three weary days in the wilderness with but one meal.

A few days later they returned, better outfitted, to map out in detail their "green gold" bonanza. Ultimately, Ball entered in his own name, having traded some tracts of land in Allegan County to Anderson for his interest, some 3,200 acres of prime white pine as well as a stand of giant white oak trees. He paid the going price for government land—$1.25 an acre.

Unfortunately, before Ball could capitalize on his find, the Panic of 1837 sent prices crashing down on the Michigan frontier, and ultimately, he made no profit.

Born in 1795 near Hebron, New Hampshire, then the western New England frontier, Ball developed the same adventuresome spirit that had characterized his pioneer ancestors. The youngest of 10 children, his youth was filled with the hard work necessary to eke an existence out of stony New England farm fields. Yearning for more education than could be acquired in the two-month "winter school" available to him, he convinced his father to allow him to leave the farm in quest of knowledge. He worked his way through a private school taught by a minister, nearby Salisbury Academy and Dartmouth College.

Following graduation, he taught school and studied law. Periodically, however, he succumbed to wanderlust. During a sailing voyage, his vessel was wrecked off the coast of Georgia, and he narrowly escaped a watery grave. Other adventures included an overland journey to Oregon in 1832, a trip to California and Hawaii and a cruise aboard a whaling vessel.

In 1836, amid a frantic mania of speculation in Michigan lands, Ball caught the fever. Three New York investors backed him in a venture in which he would travel to the Michigan frontier and purchase land in return for 25 percent of the profits.

His first trip to Michigan in August 1836 netted him little more than a valuable lesson, since he invested unwisely in some nearly worthless Monroe County swampland. But his New York investors remained confident in him, and, equipped with more gold pieces, he returned to Detroit on October 1st.

From there, he traveled over the infamously muddy Territorial Road to Kalamazoo. He marveled at the beauty of that village in comparison to the other frontier settlements he had seen. The settlers there had left the huge native oak trees standing on their lots and along the streets, and since the terrain was relatively flat, it had not been necessary to disfigure the natural lay of the land with grading.

Turning north, Ball made his way to the newly opened land office in Ionia, where he acquired maps indicating the available land in the Grand River Valley. Setting up his headquarters in the boom town of Grand Rapids, where 50-foot-wide lots sold for $2,500, he soon determined his best chances for investment lay in the wilderness to the west.

Despite his ill-fated venture in Blendon Township pine lands, Ball continued to follow the profession of landlooker, supplementing his income through the practice of law. He became so familiar with the wilderness and adept at picking the best land that his services grew in demand by the bona fide settlers who began filtering into Michigan after the worst effects of the Panic of 1837 had subsided. So ethical was he in his dealings that he earned the nickname "Honest John Ball."

Over the succeeding decades, Ball's shrewd but fair land dealings netted him a modest fortune. He purchased a large Greek Revival house, originally constructed in 1838, on Grand Rapid's East Fulton Street. There, apart from the frequent trips he took to distant parts of the world, he resided until his death in 1884.

His will granted the original 40-acre tract of what became John Ball Park to the city he loved and helped build—a fitting memorial to one of Michigan's most beloved landlookers.

Port Sheldon, The Lost Metropolis

*Broadside advertising the Ottawa House, which opened at
Port Sheldon in 1837.*

The whale oil lamps at the Ottawa House burned into the wee hours throughout the summer of 1837. From within that most luxurious hostelry in Michigan wafted the strains of melodeon and violin music, punctuated by popping champagne corks, clinking glasses and witty repartee, as gaily dressed gentlemen and ladies gambled and gamboled.

None among the hordes of speculators, "raving with land mania," flocking to the new state of Michigan were more certain they had found their fortunes than those who celebrated nightly in the Ottawa House, the social center of Port Sheldon. Situated near the mouth of Pigeon Creek, halfway between present-day Holland and Grand Haven, it was an oasis of civilization plunked down in the midst of a howling wilderness. Nevertheless, its proprietors confidently expected it to soon replace Detroit as the economic hub of the Great Lakes.

In 1835, a coterie of investors with more dollars than sense formed a joint stock company to found a city in western Michigan. That settlement, they envisioned, would become the shipping center for the agricultural products and lumber of the Great Lakes region and a marketplace for distribution of Eastern manufactured goods. Saunders Coates, editor of the *Mobile Register;* S. Taylor of Philadelphia; and A.J. Judson of New Orleans were the moving force behind the Port Sheldon Co.

The syndicate received financial backing from the National Bank of Philadelphia, whose cashier happened to be related to Judson. That institution was one of the so called "pet banks" that President Andrew Jackson had designated to receive the U.S. treasury deposits he had removed from the Bank of the United States in 1833. Jackson thus sought to hamstring Nicholas Biddle, conservative president of the bank, and to promote "easy money." The various pet banks were also authorized to issue unlimited paper money backed by little beyond their good name.

The Port Sheldon Co. established offices at Philadelphia,

72

New Orleans and other cities to promote the venture and recruit colonists. By the spring of 1836, everything was in readiness except the selection of the site.

Originally, the company opted for the mouth of the Grand River. Unfortunately, the Rev. William Ferry, who had founded the village of Grand Haven there, adamantly refused to sell out. That left only two other inferior locations on the lake in southern Michigan that had not already been gobbled up by rival speculators, the mouths of Pigeon Creek and Black River.

For some reason, the company passed up the Black River site, where Holland would be founded in 1847, for Pigeon Creek. Perhaps they were motivated by the prospect of harvesting the enormous flocks of passenger pigeons that nested nearby and gave the creek its name. In any event, the partners purchased 600 acres, nearly one square mile, of government land there at the going price of $1.25 an acre.

In the fall of 1836, an advance party of surveyors, engineers and carpenters floated down the Grand River in rafts and then made their way along Lake Michigan to the site. The main party of colonists sailed from Port Huron on the "Vindicator" and arrived shortly thereafter. The vessel's hold was loaded to the hatches with provisions, tools, precut lumber for 30 dwellings and more than an ample stock of the jug liquor required at frontier construction sites. The colonists comprised a motley array of approximately 300 men, including European fortune hunters, Army veterans, a few skilled artisans, and a goodly number of gamblers, barflies and profligates from moneyed Eastern families.

Nevertheless, those who would, set to work with a flourish. They cleared and surveyed a 160-acre plat, graded streets, laid wooden sidewalks and stalked out over 3,400 lots. Within six months, 15 buildings stood complete, including a large general store that stocked fashionable items rarely seen on the frontier. Soon, the finest sawmill in the state began buzzing its way through mountains of logs.

73

Port Sheldon Co. employees next constructed a gravel road to Grand Haven, the first such thoroughfare in the western part of the state. In expectation of a projected railroad that was to connect Port Sheldon with Port Huron, they cleared and graded two miles of railroad right-of-way and erected an elaborate depot. They also dredged a deep channel through a nasty sand bar to Lake Michigan and installed a costly lighthouse.

Some 300 residents, practically all company employees, enjoyed a good life at Port Sheldon, while it lasted. They were well-paid, well-fed and well-supplied with Eastern luxuries. They maintained a boat club where, dressed in fancy costumes, they sailed a classy yacht, the Memee (Ottawa for pigeon), and staged regattas and rowing contests.

The Ottawa House dominated the settlement. A two-story wooden structure, 60 x 120 feet in size, it was completed at a cost of $60,000 in an era when laborers counted themselves fortunate to earn 10 cents an hour. Six huge Grecian pillars supported its portico, giving it the appearance of a southern mansion. Innkeeper Charles T. Badger advertised the grand opening of his opulent hotel in Philadelphia and New York papers, promising patrons the opportunity to sample "wines and liquors of superior quality and choice brands." Numerous celebrities enjoyed Badger's hospitality including Morgan Lewis, former New York governor, and Louis of Baillet, a Belgian count. "Several fair and gentle ladies from eastern cities" who arrived in 1840 were honored with a grand ball.

By that time, however, the handwriting was on the wall for Port Sheldon. The "wild cat" currency printed by Jackson's pet banks and numerous state-chartered institutions had caused an inflationary spiral of epic proportions. In an effort to stem the flow, Jackson had issued on July 11, 1836, the Specie Circular that required government lands to be paid for in gold or silver.

The Specie Circular burst the speculative bubble and helped trigger the financial panic of 1837. The Port Shel-

74

don proprietors had already learned to their dismay that the sand-clogged channel connecting the city with the lake could not be kept open, and the ensuing depression ended what limited prospects remained.

The company paid off its employees, dismantled the sawmill, loaded up everything movable and abandoned the whole project. The last guest signed the register of the Ottawa House on March 1, 1842. Most of the other buildings were eventually dismantled for their lumber by the Dutch colonists who settled Holland.

In 1859, the southeast corner of the Ottawa House collapsed, and within a few years, the entire structure lay a heap of ruins. By the turn of the century, all traces of the city that was to be the metropolis of Michigan had disappeared.

Willy and the Wolf

*Hair-raising rendition of Willy and his wolfen mother
as depicted in an 1886 Battle Creek publication*

William Bodell felt a cold prickle of fear run down his spine as he glanced from where his children played happily before the hearth to the big gray wolf-skin robe draped across the bed. He shuddered slightly and began his story.

He was a toddler when his family emigrated from New York state to Michigan Territory. His father, John Bodell, had picked a promising site in the Grand River Valley, deep in the wilderness and some 10 miles from the nearest neighbors. It was late summer when the Bodells arrived in their covered wagon. They immediately began building a log cabin. That completed, Bodell set out a trapline, intending to provide for his family through the sale of furs and by hunting until he could begin farming the next spring.

Returning from a hunt one fine Indian summer day with a brace of wild turkeys slung over his shoulder, he surprised a huge she-wolf with her whelp. The snarling wolf positioned herself between the man and her offspring and slowly retreated. Bodell raised his muzzle loader and fired, but he missed the big wolf and killed the whelp instead. With a "howl almost human in its agony," the wolf sprang at him. He manage to club her unconscious with the butt of his rifle.

By then, it was growing dark. Having seen other wolf tracks in the vicinity, Bodell left the wolves as they lay and made a dash for his cabin. He related the adventure to his wife, vowing to never again kill a young animal with its mother as "that terrible howl of anguish yet rang in his ears."

When Bodell made the rounds of his trapline the next morning, he found the body of the whelp where he had shot it, but the old wolf was gone. After checking his traps, he returned home by a different route. As he neared the cabin, his terror-stricken wife rushed out to him, sobbing "Willie!"

She had left the child playing near the cabin door while she went to the spring for a pail of water. Returning, she found Willie gone and the ground covered with huge tracks.

Bodell unleashed his two big hounds, who soon picked up the scent. He raced through the woods after them as they headed for the spot where he had shot the young wolf. There, a blood-chilling scene awaited him.

The wolf apparently had adopted the man-child in place of her own dead offspring. Having carried Willie to her lair unharmed, she would, in maternal instinct, fight to the finish to protect her own. The hounds attacked. A terrific fight erupted as the snarling she-wolf held her ground, while ripping gaping wounds in the big dogs. Bodell feared Willie would be torn to pieces in the melee.

He took careful aim, fired, and when the smoke cleared, the wolf lay dead. So close had been the combatants that the bullet had passed through one of the dog's ears. But the child was safe, and "a humble cabin never held more thankful hearts than offered praise to God that night." Willie grew to manhood warmed at night by a bed robe fashioned from his would-be mother's hide.

From the ancient Roman legends of Romulus and Remus to Rudyard Kipling's *The Jungle Book,* literature abounds with tales of wolf-raised human children. The story of Willie and the wolf appeared in a Christmas annual published in Battle Creek in 1886. Whether it actually happened or was concocted before a flickering fire in a frontier cabin while wolves howled in the night is certainly open to conjecture.

But one fact is certain. Those who first braved the Michigan wilderness knew wolves well, and they waged a relentless war against the dreaded wild canines. Modern advocates of the theory that wolves will not attack man ought to read the records penned by Michigan pioneers.

In 1836, a party of Jackson County settlers, for example, found the scattered remains of an Indian. Nearby lay the bodies of three wolves he had slain with his hatchet before the rest dragged him down.

Although few, if any, white settlers actually got devoured alive by wolves, there are numerous close calls on record. In the early 1820's, a man named Jacoks fought off a wolf pack that attacked him and his oxen while he was traveling from Detroit to Wyandotte one winter night. He narrowly escaped by clubbing them off with a sled stake.

William Osband, who pioneered near Livonia in Wayne County in 1825, was attacked by a lone wolf while searching for the family cow one Sunday morning. He also succeeded in vanquishing the wolf with a club.

Then, there is the case of O.S. Whitmore, a logging boss who was treed by wolves in the white pine forest near the headwaters of the Manistee River. He had fought the attacking pack off with a hatchet, but in the scuffle, his lantern broke and was extinguished in the snow. Whitmore ran for a nearby tree and got partway up it before a wolf chomped onto the heel of his boot. He kicked with all his might, and luckily, the heel came loose in the wolf's mouth. A gang of his lumberjacks rescued him later.

Other similar adventures, some verifiable, other dubious, enliven the pages of Michigan's historical record. Most, however, testify to wolf depredations against livestock. Sheep, swine, chickens, and even oxen were often killed by wolves. Wolf packs sometimes went into a killing frenzy and wantonly slaughtered entire herds of animals during an attack.

Early Michigan settlers encountered two varieties of wild canines they called wolves. The smaller brush wolves were actually coyotes. The much larger gray or timber wolves normally weighed between 70 and 100 pounds. Prize specimens might double that size. Once common throughout the North America continent, timber wolves were driven before the white man's advance.

Michigan proved no exception. The territorial legislature established bounties on wolves, and one of the first official acts of most township boards was to decree wolf bounties varying from $1 to $8. Wolf bounties, verified by the beast's scalp, provided a welcome addition to hard-pressed pioneer budgets. Settlers eagerly hunted or trapped them with deadfalls, baited pens and steel traps.

Some settlements staged elaborate wolf hunts in which every male citizen felt obligated to join. A Plymouth youth earned an unenviable niche in that settlement's annuals by deserting his post during a major wolf drive. The pack bolted through that breech in the ranks. He had been stationed, it seems, in proximity to the cabin of a young damsel for whom he harbored amorous longings. While the couple spooned, the wolves escaped.

Michigan's wolf population enjoyed few such lucky breaks. They were soon hunted to extinction in settled districts. In 1868, for example, the Branch County Board of Supervisors ordered an $8 payment for the final wolf to be killed in that county. Saginaw County claims the honor of harboring the last wolf in the Lower Peninsula. It was killed in 1909.

There were plenty of wolves left in the Upper Peninsula, but the state bounty, which eventually reached $20 for females and $15 for males, continued to take its yearly toll. As late as 1939, 34 wolf scalps were redeemed for bounty. When the bounty was finally eliminated in 1960, fewer than 20 wolves remained in the Upper Peninsula.

In 1949, however, a pack had crossed the ice from Canada and established itself on Isle Royale. With the possible exception of a few isolated specimens living in the remote regions of the Upper Peninsula, the Isle Royale pack is the last of Michigan's wild timber wolves.

Douglass Houghton, Little Giant of Geology

Douglass Houghton as painted by his long time friend, Alvah Bradish.

The old settler stepped back and looked the young stranger up and down. Short and bird-like in his movements and dressed in a weather-worn gray coat, its big pockets bulging with rocks, a battered broad-brimmed hat and a pair of scuffed knee-high boots, he had suddenly appeared out of the northern woods, hundreds of miles from civilization, to pepper the pioneer with questions about the area's streams, trees, mineral deposits and wildlife.

Annoyed by the apparent nosiness of the ill-dressed vagabond, the farmer cut him short with, "You had better go and see old Dr. Houghton, of Detroit; he knows all about such things and has more time to spare than I do!"

The stranger never did tell the peeved pioneer that he was Dr. Douglass Houghton! He was satisfied to salt that incident away among the repertoire of humorous stories with which he regaled listeners around many a backwoods campfire as well as in Detroit's most fashionable salons.

Affectionately known to fellow "Wolverines" as "the little doctor," "the boy geologist of Michigan" and "our Dr. Houghton," he had energy, a range of achievements and popularity that few, if any, of the giants who cradled the state through its formative period could match.

Born in Troy, New York, on September 21, 1809, the son of a lawyer, Houghton moved with his family at an early age to Fredonia on the western New York frontier. A frail, diminutive child, he developed an early passion for the scientific study of nature. When not reading in his father's extensive library, he roamed the surrounding countryside exploring the mysteries of geology, botany and zoology. The family dog, Prince, found the boy's experiments with electricity a shocking experience.

At the age of 15, Houghton and another youth constructed a primitive gun-powder factory. Their venture went well until a pan of the powder blew up in Houghton's face, temporarily blinding him and scarring him for life. After recovering from that accident, Houghton continued his studies at a local academy.

Following graduation, he enrolled in the renowned Rensselaer Polytechnic School at Troy. Over the succeeding four years, Houghton endured a rigorous academic regimen featuring school days that began at 4:30 a.m. and continued well into the evening. Finally, in 1829, he received his Bachelor of Arts degree and that, with the exception of the study of medicine, concluded his formal education.

Impressed with Houghton's abilities, Prof. Amos Eaton, principal of Rensselaer and one of the country's leading educators, selected him to join the faculty.

In 1830, a group of culture-starved Detroiters, including Territorial Gov. Lewis Cass; John Biddle; and Lucius Lyon, territorial delegate to Congress, launched a campaign to bring a lecturer on chemistry, botany and geology to their city. When Lyon visited Eaton to solicit his recommendation, he promptly introduced his protege, Houghton, as an ideal candidate.

Although initially startled at the thought of a mere teenager lecturing to well-educated adults, Lyon was convinced after interviewing him. Houghton jumped at the opportunity, and in November 1830, he arrived in Detroit with his scientific apparatus and only 10 cents in his pocket.

Houghton's initial 26 lectures on chemistry, for which he charged $2 per person for the entire series, were an immediate success. He soon became one of the most popular men in Detroit, and he decided to cast his lot with the frontier peninsulas he grew to love.

Returning briefly to New York the following year, Houghton received his medical license in time to accept appointment as a surgeon and botanist to the federal expedition to discover the source of the Mississippi River headed by his friend Henry Rowe Schoolcraft. Houghton's report on the new plants discovered by the expedition won him further scientific acclaim. Over the course of the arduous canoe voyage, he also gave smallpox vaccinations to hundreds of Indians. And, most significantly, he first learned of the presence of copper in the Keweenaw region.

Upon his return to Detroit in the fall of 1832, Houghton hung out his shingle, and he soon enjoyed a thriving practice. He further won the affection of Detroit citizens by risking his life ministering to rich and poor alike during the cholera epidemics that ravaged the city in 1832 and 1834.

Houghton married Harriet Stevens, a childhood friend, in 1833 and, to supplement family income, began speculating in Detroit real estate. Eventually, that endeavor proved so profitable that he abandoned his medical practice.

When Michigan finally entered the Union on January 26, 1837, Houghton became one of the leading advocates for a state geological survey. A month later, the state Legislature approved a bill authorizing an "accurate and complete geological survey of the state," and Houghton was appointed state geologist with a first year's budget of $3,000. Houghton abandoned most of his other activities and even turned down the presidency of the incipient University of Michigan to immerse himself wholeheartedly in the survey work. During his first year's work, he explored many of the major rivers in the Lower Peninsula.

By 1838, however, the effects of the Panic of 1837 had begun to undermine the state's grandiose development program, including funding for the geological survey. The survey might well have been completely curtailed had not Houghton bailed it out with his own private resources.

In the summer of 1839, he began survey operations in the Upper Peninsula. Although other aspects of the survey, including selection of valuable salt springs granted the state by the federal government and detailed maps of the southern tiers of counties, received his attention, most of his energies over the succeeding five years went toward exploring and promoting the rich mineral lands of the Upper Peninsula. His reports on the Keweenaw copper country inspired a frenzied rush for the red metal.

In addition to his geological activities, Houghton cam-

84

paigned for temperance in Detroit, served as president of that city's Board of Education and retained a professorship at the University of Michigan. In 1841, while in the wilderness intent on his survey work, he received notification that in his absence he had been elected mayor of Detroit. He came within a hair's breath of being nominated as a gubernatorial candidate while similarly engaged in 1844.

With the leading men in the state his close friends, his name revered by the people, his Upper Peninsula survey work nearing completion and his political future bright, Houghton's star was clearly on the ascendancy during the fall of 1845.

Suddenly, fate intervened in the form of the unpredictable nature of the big lake worshiped by the Ojibwa as Gitchee Gummee. On October 13, 1845, while Houghton and four others were en route from Eagle Harbor to Eagle River on the Keweenaw Peninsula, a sudden storm struck. The huge waves overturned their Mackinaw boat and Houghton went down to a watery grave. His corpse was found on the beach the following spring.

The entire state went into mourning for the talented young man who had given his all for his adopted state. A city, a county and a lake honor his name.

Angelique's Isle Royale Nightmare

A poem about Angelique published in 1892 included an artist's stylized rendition of the heroine.

Not even the awesome grandeur of the curtain of colors shimmering across the northern sky, the "dancing spirits" of the aurora borealis, could help Angelique forget her plight. Marooned on a small ice-bound island off the coast of Isle Royale without a scrap of food, the young Indian woman was starving to death.

Sometimes, she longed for the same peaceful death that had come to her husband, Charlie Mott, a gaunt frozen corpse in a nearby lodge. Angelique no longer prayed for release from the "craving that gnawed within like a wolf." But she did pray most fervently, on her knees, for deliverance from the awful thought that seized her when the hunger raged the worst—the temptation "to take Charlie and make soup of him."

She had not been trained by the black robes in vain. She knew it would be a mortal sin to desecrate a human body—especially that of her husband. She did not want to do it, but what she feared the most was that driven out of her mind by the hunger, she would regain her senses "in the very act of eating him."

The daughter of an Ojibwa chief, Shawano of Sault Ste. Marie, Angelique had grown into a robust maiden, renowned for her beauty and extraordinary strength. Once, a Frenchman bet her that she could not carry a barrel of pork to the summit of a nearby hill and back. She promptly won the wager with ease and upon completing that feat, "volunteered to carry the barrel up again with the Frenchman on top of it."

It was another Frenchman, Mott, of whom his fellow voyageurs knew only that "handsome he was, and wore a shirt of blue," who captured Angelique's heart. Married in June 1845, they moved to La Pointe, an ancient settlement on Madeline Island in the Apostle Islands.

At that time, the Keweenaw country to the east was experiencing a frenzied search for the red metal that rivaled the later California Gold Rush. Angelique's troubles began when some copper prospectors from Detroit, "big bugs" as she called them, arrived in La Pointe on the schooner Algonquin later that month. At their request, Mott and his bride accompanied them on a scouting expedition to Isle Royale.

While walking along the beach, Angelique discovered a large mass of native copper shining in the water. Ecstatic over the find, the Detroit prospectors hired the Motts at $30 per month to guard the claim until they could return and establish a mining operation. The Motts sailed on the Algonquin to Sault Ste. Marie, where they planned to lay in an ample supply of provisions.

There, however, they met Cyrus Mendenhall, a prominent copper prospector and guide, who persuaded them not to purchase their provisions at the Sault but to save the heavy freight costs and buy them from him at La Pointe. But upon reaching La Pointe, they discovered that he had lied to them and had no provisions available. Nevertheless, the Motts succeeded in borrowing from the mission there a half barrel of flour, a few pounds of beans, and six pounds of butter that "smelt badly and was white like lard."

Against Angelique's counsel, Mott, "over-persuaded by Mendenhall," agreed to go to Isle Royale anyway. Mendenhall promised to send a bateau with provisions within a few weeks and that at the end of three months he would return in a ship to take them off the island.

On July 1, 1845, he landed the Motts on a small island at the mouth of Rock Harbor on the northeast tip of Isle Royale with only their miserable stock of provisions, a small birch-bark canoe and a fish net. The Lake Superior Crusoes lived on the fish they were able to net until the end of summer when the canoe was wrecked and net ruined during a fierce storm.

Then came long days of anxiously scanning the horizon for the promised rescue ship. But neither the bateau nor schooner ever arrived. By December 20, their supplies were exhausted. It was bitter cold, and a heavy snow had fallen. They had no snowshoes or tools to dig in the frozen ground for roots. All that was left was to shiver before a little fire in the lodge they had constructed and draw their belts tighter and tighter.

Mott grew weaker and weaker until he lost his mind. One day, he began sharpening his knife on a whetstone. Glaring at his wife, he told her "he was tired of being hungry, he would kill a sheep—something to eat he must have." All day and all night, she watched him, not daring to fall asleep for fear he would spring at her any moment. Finally, she managed to wrest the knife away, and eventually Mott came out of his "fever fit."

Angelique watched him "sink away and dry up until there was nothing left of him but skin and bones." He died so quietly that she could not tell "just when the breathe did leave his body." She dutifully washed him and laid him out, but she could not dig a grave in the frozen ground and "could not bear to throw him into the snow." For three days, she remained with the body, which "seemed almost like company" to her.

Finally, fearing that if she kept up the heat in the lodge "he would spoil," she managed to construct another small hut where she moved the fire. Somehow, she lived on, with the flickering flames for companionship and only bark to fill her stomach. When the hunger raged the worst, she swallowed a pinch of salt.

A week or so later came "the worst trouble of all," the fear that she would lose her sanity as her husband had and that she would find herself eating him. She prayed all night long "that the good God would give me something to eat lest the ever-increasing temptation would come over me at last."

The very next morning when she threw open the door to her hut, she spied for the first time some rabbit tracks. She frantically tore a lock of hair out of her head and began plaiting it into a snare. She soon caught one and ravenously ripped off its skin and wolfed it raw.

And so it went throughout the long northern winter. By spring, she had "torn half the hair out of her head to make snares" but had never managed to catch more than one rabbit a week. Her lot improved when, early in March, Angelique found a canoe that had washed ashore, repaired it, and fashioned a crude net from strips of its sail.

One May morning, she had the exceptional fortune to net four mullets and was in the process of preparing them for breakfast when a gunshot rang out. She nearly fainted; and when she tried to run down to the landing, her knees gave way, and she tumbled to the ground.

She recovered in time to arrive at the landing just as a rescue party was alighting. The first man out of the boat was none other than Mendenhall, who calmly shook hands with Angelique and asked, "Where is Charlie?"

When Angelique told him that her husband had died of starvation, Mendenhall began "to cry and to try to explain things." He sobbed that "he had sent off a bateau with provisions and didn't see why they didn't get to us." The crew later told Angelique that it was all a lie.

Angelique was "too glad to get back to my mother to do anything—I thought his own conscience ought to punish him more than I could do."

The woman who "seemed to be fashioned to demonstrate to what reaches of suffering the human frame could go and still withstand the shock" later worked as a cook for a Marquette family. More than once, she woke the household with her nightmare screams: "Going to eat my Charlie!"

Angelique died at Sault Ste. Marie in 1874. The scene of the tragedy still carries the name Mott Island.

The Potters of Potterville

Theodore Edgar Potter as a Union captain in 1864.

S tifling her sobs, Diana Potter hitched her two-year-old son, James, from one hip to the other and cast a final lingering look at the fresh grave that scarred the corner of the wheat field. Then, she and her seven children crossed the field to their log shanty at the site of what would become the Eaton County community of Potterville.

Bereft of the head of their family, who at the age of 48 had succumbed to the effects of overworking himself in the same wheat field where he now lay in eternal rest, the Potters faced a bleak future. It was July 26, 1846, and the ring of the settler's axe and the bark of the hunter's rifle had just begun to be heard in that section of Michigan. The foreboding hardwood giants that ringed the Potter's seven-acre clearing stretched endlessly in all directions.

Offered an opportunity to return to western New York to live with relatives, practically the only form of welfare assistance available in pioneer society, Potter declined, replying that "all she had to live for was her seven children and that as she had moved 15 times since her marriage she did not intend to move again as long as she could keep the family together."

Her 14-year-old son, Theodore, would relate the family drama in an autobiography published in 1913. And of all the many adventures he recorded, including an overland trek to the California gold fields, Indian fighting, a stint with Gen. William Walker's filibustering expedition to Nicaragua and service in the Civil War, none is more fascinating than the story of his childhood struggles for survival on the Michigan frontier.

Born in Saline, Washtenaw County, in 1832, to a father who, like many another pioneer, always saw greener fields beckoning to the west, Theodore Potter moved with his family to the unbroken forests of Eaton County in 1844.

Using only an axe, adz, saw and auger, the Potters constructed a two-room log shanty. Not a nail was used in the process, and the only cash outlay went for the purchase of two small glass windows. The walls consisted of straight beech and elm logs, the thickest laid to the front so as to provide a slope for the roof. Split basswood logs, hollowed out like troughs then laid in alternate overlapping rows without rafters or shingles, covered the roof. Puncheon logs, round on the bottom and hewn on the top, served as the floor. Two huge fireplaces cut through the log walls and stick chimneys plastered with clay offered the sole cooking and heating facilities.

The Potters' only cash, $100 received from the sale of the previous farm, went to purchase their 80-acre homestead at the land office in Ionia. Despite suffering an attack of measles, the family managed to clear seven acres their first winter. In the spring, they planted corn, potatoes, pumpkins and squash; following a bountiful harvest in the fall, three acres were sown with winter wheat. Over-exuberance in cutting that wheat with a sickle under the hot July sun proved the elder Potter's downfall.

Survival on the Michigan frontier, however, left no time for prolonged grieving. The day after their father's funeral, the Potter children carried the wheat to their barn and threshed out ten bushels with flails. Theodore hauled it, along with five bushels of corn, 10 miles to the nearest gristmill on the Grand River, returning with enough flour and cornmeal to last the family for three months.

The Potters supplemented their crops with whatever wild game they had the good fortune to secure. While retrieving the family cow from the woods one morning, 14-year-old Theodore and his dog encountered a large buck deer. The deer attacked the dog; and when the teenager ran to help it, the deer turned on him. Dodging from tree to tree, he managed to grab an oak stick with which he eventually clubbed the buck to death. The family enjoyed venison for an entire week, and the story of the boy's adventure found its way into newspapers throughout the state. A later hunting experience proved less fortunate. Mistaking the family cow for a deer, he eliminated their much-needed milk supply.

Nuts, berries and edible plants also helped vary the tedious frontier diet. One spring, the Potters hollowed out split ash logs to make troughs, tapped a nearby stand of maple trees and succeeded in producing 800 pounds of sugar. What sugar did not go for home consumption was bartered for "store bought" luxuries.

Wild honey also proved a valuable prize. Hollow bee trees were occasionally discovered by accident, but sophisticated bee hunters practiced the art of geometry. A small wooden box with a sliding glass top containing honey was left in the sun for bees to find. After gorging themselves with honey, the insects made a "bee-line" for their hive. The bee hunter marked their line of flight with blazes on the trees. Then, closing the lid of the box with bees inside, it was moved several hundred feet to one side. Where the flight of the released bees crossed the previous bee line revealed the exact location of the hive. Setting a smudge fire at the base of the tree and chopping it down, a successful hunter might secure several hundred pounds of honey.

Ashes, however, comprised the primary cash crop harvested by the Potters and other pioneers who settled in the hardwood forests. With the assistance of adult laborers, the family spent much of the winter chopping down giant oak, ash, maple and walnut trees. The logs were rolled into huge piles and set afire. The resulting ashes were converted into "black salts" at a neighbor's ashery, then hauled in wagons to the nearest railroad depot at Marshall and shipped to Buffalo for processing into baking soda and other products.

Many a settler paid for the entire cost of his land through the sale of ashes. Although in retrospect, that practice proved a tragic waste of valuable timber, there was little market for hardwood on the frontier; and the land needed to be cleared for cultivation.

One way or another, by 1852, the Potter family had not only survived the worst of the tough times but managed to increase their land holdings. No longer desperately needed on the farm, Theodore Potter was permitted to follow his dream of seeking his fortune among the California gold fields. Thus began a series of adventures that would carry him across the continent several times and win him martial glory.

Diana Potter spent the remainder of her life on the homestead she had worked so hard to preserve. At the age of 80, she proudly wrote: "I kept my family with me until they became men and women, and neither of my five boys, to my knowledge, have ever used liquor or tobacco, and all have good homes and families."

Three years later, she died in the community which bears her family's name.

Laura Haviland, Michigan's "Mother of Philanthropy"

Slave hunters from Tennessee attempt to force Laura Haviland to hand over their prey in 1846.

Trembling with rage, the slave hunters poked their six-shooters at the 37-year-old Quaker lady from Adrian who had dared to foil their plot to shanghai a runaway black family. Looking down from the open window of an Erie & Kalamazoo Railroad coach, Laura S. Haviland ignored the ugly bores of the weapons leveled but two feet from her face and calmly told the desperate pair, "Men, I fear neither your weapons nor your threats; they are powerless. You are not at home—you are not in Tennessee. As for your property, I have none of it about me or on my premises."

It was mid-November 1846 at Sylvania, Ohio, near the Michigan border. The property in question, the James Hamilton family, had been lured from the sanctuary of Haviland's underground railroad station near Adrian through a series of bogus letters entreating the runaway slaves to visit the deathbed of a Southern friend.

"Smelling a rat," Haviland had accompanied the blacks to Toledo where, after exposing the fraud, she had ushered her friends onto a train headed back to Adrian. The slave hunters, John P. Chester and his son Thomas, had sneaked aboard the train, intending to make a last-ditch effort to capture the family worth thousands of dollars in Tennessee.

Their chance came when the train halted at Sylvania in order to sand the ice-covered tracks. But their guns and threats had no effect on the prim little widow. She calmly faced them down until the conductor came to her aid. The cowardly slave hunters fled to a nearby woods and the last that was seen of them "were their heels fast receding in the thicket."

Haviland recounted that, and the many other adventures she experienced during her more than four decades spent assisting downtrodden blacks, in an autobiography published in 1881. The copy before me carries an inscription in her own hand: "No word, or tear of sympathy with the poor, and oppressed, is ever in vain." That philosophy guided her throughout her long life.

97

Born December 20, 1808, in Leeds County, Ontario, Laura was the eldest of the eight children of Daniel and Sene Smith. Her father was a minister and her mother an elder in the Society of Friends. Originally from Vermont, the Smiths moved back to the U.S. in 1815, settling in Niagara County, New York.

At the age of 16, Laura married Charles Haviland, a young Quaker farmer. In 1829, they immigrated to the Quaker settlement established in Raisin Township, Lenawee County. Three years later, the Havilands became charter members of Michigan's first antislavery society, organized by Elizabeth Margaret Chandler, another noted Quaker abolitionist who had moved to the Adrian area in 1830.

When the more conservative hierarchy of the Society of Friends objected to their radical abolitionist activity, the Havilands and 18 friends and relatives left the church. By 1844, Laura Haviland had become a minister in the Wesleyan Methodist Church, which had broken with the Methodist Episcopal Church over the slavery issue.

In the meantime, their heartfelt concern for the orphans and indigent children who led a miserable existence in the Lenawee County poorhouse spurred the Havilands to establish a school for the poor on their farm in 1837. Two years later, it became the River Raisin Institute, a manual-labor school patterned after Oberlin College and open to all regardless of sex or color. At that time, it was the only school in the state "that would open its door to a colored person."

The River Raisin Institute and the Haviland's home also frequently served as havens for fugitive slaves en route to Canada. Yet, despite the hundreds of white students whose racial prejudice "melted away" through attendance at the institute, the school was widely regarded throughout the state as a "nigger den."

Tragedy struck the community during the spring of 1845 in the form of a streptococcus epidemic. Haviland's husband, both parents, a sister, her youngest child and many close friends died within weeks. Nevertheless, the widow managed to support her six surviving offspring as well as devote more of her energies to the antislavery movement.

Haviland ultimately placed the River Raisin Institute under the management of others while she traveled throughout the nation delivering fiery abolitionist speeches. She made numerous forays into the South, fearlessly campaigning against slavery. She also became an operative on the Underground Railroad, leading fugitive slaves through Ohio, Indiana and Michigan to sanctuary in Canada.

Despite the $3,000 reward placed on her head by slave owners, she eluded capture. When the Civil War broke out in 1861, she also began visiting army hospitals and prison camps.

In 1864, she received the first salary of her life, $40-per-month stipend as an agent of the Michigan Freedmen's Aid Commission. She traveled throughout the South in that capacity, assisting ex-slaves acculturate to freedom. Under the sponsorship of the Freedmen's Aid Commission, she also converted the River Raisin Institute into a model orphanage. Although that experiment ultimately failed, she continued to campaign for the needs of orphans. Her efforts spurred the Legislature to create the State Public School for Dependent Children in Coldwater in 1871.

In conjunction with Elizabeth Comstock, another Quaker reformer from Lenawee County, Haviland went to Kansas in 1879 to work with the ex-slaves who had flocked there following the war. During the 1870's and 1880's, Haviland also became active in the woman's suffrage movement and the temperance crusade.

Haviland moved to Grand Rapids in 1893. That same year, she was honored as "the mother of philanthropy" during Michigan Day at the Columbian World's Fair.

She died in Grand Rapids at the age of 89 and was buried in the Friend's Cemetery near Adrian. In 1909,

Adrian citizens erected on the courthouse lawn a statue of Haviland as "a tribute to a life consecrated to the betterment of humanity."

Mary Day, The Blind Girl

Mary L. Day's portrait appeared in her 1859 autobiography.

Mary L. Day sat dejectedly on a log alongside a country road near Marshall, as morose a 12-year-old as could be found in all of Michigan. Ever since her mother had died six years before and she and her siblings had been scattered among families in need of child labor, her life had been one of misery and mistreatment. Now, because she had spent a Sunday attending church and playing with friends without permission, her mistress had thrown her out of the house with aught save the clothes on her back and $2 severance pay.

It was a beautiful June morning in 1848, but the fragrant wildflowers and caroling birds could little cheer the friendless orphan. When finally she arose to wander she knew not where, she fell to the ground in a faint, as was the wont of Victorian heroines.

She awoke a week later to find herself in a bed surrounded by curtains. A passing Samaritan had found her alongside the road and carried her back to his home. A physician had pronounced her case "congestion of the brain, caused by some great shock to her nervous system."

Tenderly nursed by the kind family, Mary seemed to have recovered after several weeks. But, alas, later that summer, she suffered a relapse, inflamed eyelids and severe pain in her eyes. Within 24 hours, she had been rendered permanently sightless.

Mary detailed the sad story of her life in *Incidents in the Life of a Blind Girl,* first published in Baltimore in 1859. Throughout the 19th century, the sale of such autobiographies was a common method by which blind, deaf and dumb or crippled individuals attempted to supplement their meager budgets and achieve a degree of self-sufficiency. Graced with a frontispiece of her likeness, Day's 206-page volume went through at least four editions. Far more than a literary souvenir, however, her autobiography documents the sad state of affairs when the care and protection of orphans and the physically handicapped depended solely on the goodness of human nature.

Born in Baltimore, Maryland, in 1836, Mary had immigrated with her family to the frontier community of White Pigeon while "but a babe in her mother's arms." There, her father eked out a livelihood as a tinsmith.

Six months later, the Days moved to Shermantown, as Sturgis was then known, and soon thereafter, their prospects brightened with the unexpected payment of a Baltimore debt. Day purchased a beautiful tract of land on the shores of Silver Lake, 10 miles south of Coldwater in Kinderhook Township, and the family moved into a two-story log house there.

Soon, however, the hard times that struck Michigan following the financial panic of 1837, necessitated Day's seeking employment in Jonesville, approximately 40 miles away. He stayed in Jonesville over the winter while his family managed a precarious existence at their wilderness homestead, far from the nearest neighbor.

Ultimately, Day was forced to sell his farm and the family joined him in Jonesville, where his wife took ill and died. Unable or unwilling to care for his children alone, Day secured foster homes for them among various pioneer families throughout the region. Mary's unfortunate lot fell to join a stern household near Homer in Calhoun County. The shrewish woman of the house repeatedly beat and otherwise abused the six-year-old for trivial infractions.

Once, when left to prepare Sunday dinner while the family attended church, she misgauged the amount of vegetables required. Her mistress returned with several guests, inspected the kitchen, then kindly beckoned the little girl into another room. Grabbing her by the hair, as Mary recalled, the cold-hearted wretch "beat me first on one side of my head, and then on the other," after which she stifled the child's cries with a hand over her mouth. Mary took four years of such treatment before she ran away.

Next came a series of jobs as maid in country homes, the last near Marshall, until her rude dismissal, the shock of which evidently brought on her blindness.

The myriad social welfare agencies currently charged with protecting orphans, the indigent, the blind, etc., were yet to make their appearance in Michigan of 1848, that is, with the exception of the county poorhouse, a last refuge for unfortunates suffering from poverty, senility, mental disorders, physical afflictions, and in some cases orphans. The quality of life experienced by poorhouse inmates differed widely from county to county depending on the tax base and/or the frugality of county commissioners. Some poorhouse superintendents, in fact, earned their salary in proportion to how cheaply they could feed and shelter their charges.

Mary narrowly escaped the poorhouse, but only because she happened to encounter a kind patron. As is so often the case, it happened to be a family who could least afford charity. One of the trustees responsible for committing individuals to the Calhoun County Poor House, a Mr. Cook, took pity on the blind girl and carried her in his arms to his wife, saying: "Fanny, I have brought this poor child home to live with us, we have seven children, I think we have bread enough for them and her too; take her, dear Fanny, and be a mother to her."

Mrs. Cook cheerfully welcomed Mary into the family circle as did the seven young children to whom she became a sister. They read to the blind girl, and Mrs. Cook taught her to knit. After one year of practice, she was able to knit a respectable pair of stockings. Soon, she accepted a job of doing another family's knitting at the rate of $1 a week. Over the next four years, she supported herself in that fashion.

What Mary really needed, obviously, was to attend a training school equipped to deal with the special needs of the blind. Unfortunately, Michigan had yet to create such an institution.

Actually, in 1848, the Legislature had laid the groundwork for the establishment of the Michigan Asylum for Educating the Deaf, Dumb and the Blind. Not until 1854, however, did the institution open in rented quarters in Flint. The first class consisted of 12 students, only one of whom was blind. Two years later, the school moved into its own structure.

The emphasis at Flint, apparently, was always on educating the deaf—blind students never numbered more than 25 percent of the enrollment. Finally, in 1879, the Legislature approved the establishment of a separate facility for the blind. The Michigan School for the Blind opened the following year in Lansing with an enrollment of 35. Not until 1904, however, would the Michigan Employment Institute open in Saginaw. Its objective was to train the blind for employment and self-sufficiency after graduation.

All of this came too late for Mary, the poor blind girl. Eventually, she journeyed to Baltimore where she was reconciled with well-to-do family members. After several treatments by the best "oculists" failed to restore her eyesight, she enrolled in the Maryland Institution for the Blind, a model training school located in Baltimore.

Mary proudly noted that she was a graduate of that institute in her 1859 autobiography. A sequel published 19 years later revealed that though "forever veiled the beauty of sun or flower" remained her heavy cross to bear, the blind girl from Michigan had found a devoted husband to help ease her load.

Nessmuk's Tramp Across the Peninsula

George W. Sears, alias Nessmuk.

Nessmuk took careful aim at the big, glossy-coated black bear as it sat on its haunches calmly chewing a mouthful of acorns a scant 25 yards away. The bright bead of the rifle's front sight showed plainly against the butt of his ear. One squeeze of the hair trigger and the grand trophy was his.

Then Nessmuk lowered his rifle and watched the animal leisurely amble closer, oblivious to the danger. Finally, when the near-sighted beast began sniffing around under the very tree where Nessmuk sat, he suddenly leaped to his feet, threw his hat at him and uttered a shrill "Comanche yell." The bear tumbled backward, "grunting and whining for very terror," then disappeared into the underbrush as fast as his short legs could carry him.

Unlike many a hunter of his time, Nessmuk was a true sportsman. Alone in the Michigan wilderness, somewhere between Saginaw and Muskegon, on that October day in the early 1850's, he had no conceivable use for either the bear's skin or meat. He had enjoyed the sight of the beautiful creature and had merely sighted his rifle to prove to himself how easily he could have taken a trophy. But he had concluded that, "shot down and left to taint the blessed air, he would not look as wholesome, let alone that it would be unwarrantable murder."

Nessmuk, the pen name of George W. Sears, related the bear story in a chapter about a 10-day tramp through the Michigan wilderness in his classic guide to camping, hunting and fishing lore, *Woodcraft,* first published in 1884. Sears' volume went through 13 editions by 1918, and he also published a volume of nature poems in 1887.

Born in 1821, "in a cabin on the borders of Douglas Woods, in Massachusetts," Sears later moved to Rochester, New York, where he attended school. At an early age, he developed a life-long passion for hunting, fly fishing and canoeing. What is more, at a time when most of his countrymen were lustily harvesting the continent's natural bounties with little thought of preservation, he promoted a remarkable environmentalist philosophy.

Sears offered a simple bit of poetic wisdom to the over-worked denizens of the cities where:

"Lungs are poisoned and shoulders bowed,
In the smothering reek of mill and mine;
And death stalks in on the struggling crowd—
But he shuns the shadow of oak and pine."

Sears followed his own advice and took a vacation outing to Michigan, where two old classmates from Rochester had settled. Pete Williams and family had established a homestead in the Saginaw vicinity. Joe Davis, conceivably the Joseph D. Davis who became Muskegon County's first treasurer in 1859, settled on the Muskegon River, upstream from the lumber town at its mouth.

Boarding the 391-ton steamer, the Globe, at Buffalo, Sears made an easy voyage to Lower Saginaw, as Bay City was known until 1857. From there, a half-day's jaunt on a buckboard brought him to Williams' cabin in the woods. Unfortunately, the family was down with the ague, as malaria was then called, and had no appetite for the game Sears brought in.

Having "the decency not to slaughter game for the love of killing, and leave it to rot, or hook large fish that could not be used," Sears decided to visit his other chum on the Muskegon. On the advice of an old frontiersman named Bill Hance, Sears concluded it would be possible to walk across the 100 miles of wilderness that lay between him and Davis.

Sears, who preached the gospel of traveling light, packed only a hatchet, knife, compass, blanket-bag, knapsack, a loaf of bread, two quarts of cornmeal, two pounds of pork, a pound of sugar, tea, salt, a supply of venison jerky and a tin dish. He was armed with his new Billinghurst, a prototype repeating rifle invented by a Rochester gunsmith, along with 12 rounds of ammunition, extra powder and a bullet mold.

Early one "crisp, bright October morning," he bid his

108

friends goodbye and started west on an old Indian trail Hance had pointed out. As he had expected, it soon "branched off to right and left, grew dimmer and slimmer, degenerated to a deer path, petered out to a squirrel track, ran up a tree and ended in a knot hole." Undismayed that he was alone in the wilderness, Sears followed his nose and his compass westward.

The weather was near perfect, with no annoying insects left and the autumn foliage breathtaking. "The only drawback," he recalled, "was the harassing and vexatious manner in which lakes, streams, swamps and marshes constantly persisted in getting across the way, compelling long detours."

Perhaps because most of the native Ottawa had been "removed" to Kansas and the pioneers and lumbermen had yet to make their appearance in that section of the state, Sears encountered an amazing abundance of wildlife. There was not "an hour of daylight on the trip where squirrels were not too numerous to be counted." The woods were alive with passenger pigeons, grouse, and deer, which tamely watched him at close range. "There was scarcely a day," he marveled, "when I could not have had a standing shot at a bear."

Once, while he stopped to rest, a hideous wild boar with gleaming tusks approached him but was frightened off as had been the black bear. During another rest break in heavy timber, an "army of wild turkeys," too numerous to count, marched by within 50 feet of where he sat. To his credit as a sportsman, Sears fired only three shots during the entire trip, and each time he nailed a young deer for fresh meat.

At the end of ten days, Sears emerged from the woods on the banks of the Muskegon River just as he had planned. Constructing a raft, he floated down the river to Davis' lumber mill.

Thirty years of hunting later, Sears testified that during his Michigan trip, he had seen "more game birds and animals in the time than I ever saw before or since in a whole season."

He readily admitted, however, that had he encountered bad weather or a forest fire, his trip could have easily ended in disaster. He had sage advice for any of his readers who might be "tempted to make a similar thoughtless, reckless trip — don't do it."

Daniel B. Kellogg, Ann Arbor's Clairvoyant Doctor

Daniel B. Kellogg in 1869.

Painting grotesque the faces of those who sat around the table, the flickering candle cast monstrous shadows on the walls. The coterie of young couples who had gathered at the rural Washtenaw County home of "Dr." Daniel B. Kellogg one evening in 1856 had exhausted the local gossip and craved something more exciting to do.

Someone suggested they take advantage of Kellogg's highly touted reputation as a medium and conduct a seance. Kellogg quickly determined their polarity—those with cold hands were positive, and those with moist, warm hands negative. Counting Kellogg's wife, a fledgling medium, herself, the circle was in equilibrium. All could participate—all, that is, save Kellogg's "semi-idiotic" hired man—he could only watch.

The couples sat around the table, placed their hands palms down in front of them and purged their minds of all unkind feelings, envy or jealousy. Kellogg lapsed into a trance, a spirit presence soon made itself felt and for some time the couples amused themselves by attempting to tell fortunes. Eventually, that too grew boring.

Suddenly, before Kellogg could stop him, someone at the table "formally asked the spirits if we could receive a manifestation from the Witch of Endor." Immediately, everyone experienced a strange tingling feeling like a weak electric shock, and their hands were irresistibly pressed down against the table. The women screamed and called for help, but no one could wrench their hands "from the vise-like grip of the unseen power."

The candle blew out. Then the table began to spin around the room, whirling the couples with it, and chairs were "hurled hither and thither about the room with fierce velocity," narrowly missing their heads. Doors slammed open and shut, loud raps reverberated through the walls and the windows "shook as if under the influence of a hurricane power." Meanwhile, the "poor frightened half idiot" ran from door to door vainly trying to leave the room.

The uncanny phenomena continued for some 20 minutes, then just as suddenly as it had started, it stopped. It became completely still, and the couples found they could move their hands. Expecting to find the room in shambles, someone struck a match, only to discover every article of furniture exactly where it had been. Uncertain whether they had experienced "hallucinations of mind" or "phantasm of brain" or had indeed had a close encounter with the Witch of Endor, the couples vowed to "keep silent about the visitation."

Thirteen years later, however, Kellogg broke that vow and told "the real facts" in his autobiography published in Ann Arbor. Moreover, by that time, he had parlayed his prowess at the parlor table into a lucrative livelihood as a "clairvoyant physician," able to discern the nature of and treat wide-ranging afflictions via his spirit guide, an Indian doctor known variously as Walapaca and Owosso.

Born in 1834 in a tumble-down log shanty in Washtenaw County's Pittsfield Township, Kellogg bore no relationship to the Battle Creek cereal clan. A sickly child and considered a dolt by fellow pupils who gathered at a local log schoolhouse, Kellogg, by the age of 15, had come to the realization that he "had a natural incapacity for learning." That deficiency, however, was more than made up for by his incipient clairvoyant powers. For one thing, he had gained a reputation as a "human weathercock," able to predict atmospheric changes with unerring accuracy.

Kellogg might have pursued a career as a meteorologist had he not, at the age of 18, attended a demonstration by an itinerant mesmerist. There, he found himself so thoroughly hypnotized that he ate a quid of tobacco like candy. Needles poked into his hands caused no pain.

The ease with which he could be controlled by the hypnotist opened Kellogg's eyes to the realization that he was a very sensitive individual. From there, it was but a short step to be governed by the spirits of those who had passed before.

Soon Kellogg found himself leading a double life—by

day "a shy, uneducated, hard working mechanic," by night, under spirit influences, "a remarkable intellectual prodigy." Psychic healing became his forte. The human organism was like an open book. Without any medical training, he found himself able to "locate and define every pain human flesh was heir to."

In the process, he discovered that all disease was simply "a want of equilibrium in the circulation of the vitalic principles." What is more, the old Indian spirit doctor, who for some reason took him under his wing, taught him the exact herbs that would restore the vitalic equilibrium. While under trance, Kellogg was frequently heard to converse with him—in a strange Indian dialogue.

Kellogg cured acquaintances for free for several years and, as his fame spread, increasing numbers of "poor diseased humanity, aching, groaning, limping, coughing, dying" thronged his home. He began charging a small fee, and still they came. He raised his fee to $1 for consultation, quit his mechanic's job and still the lame and the halt stumbled to his rural dwelling.

Soon, he found he was able to focus his psychic powers across hundreds of miles, when the weather permitted. As a result, patients needed merely post him their name and a few other bits of vital information, enclose $1 in the envelope and he would speed back a form letter diagnosing the case and prescribing medicines—available strictly through him at additional fees. Removal of cancers became a specialty.

Business prospered to the extent that, in 1865, he moved his abode to Ann Arbor, "the great northwestern emporium of medical knowledge." There, he established Dr. Kellogg's Medical Works in a four-story brick structure on Broadway near the Huron River. During the following decade, Kellogg expanded his services with the aid of his wife and an older brother, Leverett, to include a variety of patent medicines, including "Kellogg's Liver Invigorator" and "Kellogg's Magic Red Drops."

Sadly, and apparently despite his rapport with the here-after, Kellogg died at the age of 42 in 1876—leaving his many long-suffering patients without a ghost of a chance of getting their money back.

The Perils of
Pauline Cushman

Pauline Cushman toasts Jeff Davis.

Confederate Gen. Braxton Bragg moved closer to his captive, scrutinizing her beautiful dark eyes for any sign of betrayal. "If found guilty, you will be hanged," he said.

Pauline Cushman felt the blood drain from her face. Her hands twitched as she mastered the urge to clasp her neck in protection. But she who had treaded the boards of New York stages, who had fearlessly faced angry audiences well-armed with ripe vegetables, would now play her part well, to the end if need be. She tossed her head and said, "Come now, General, I don't think that I would prove a very ornamental object, dangling at the end of a rope."

But pretty Pauline could not act her way out of this plight. The evidence, drawings of rebel fortifications found hidden between the soles of her boots, was too strong. For 10 days in June 1863, her fate hung in the balance. Then a Confederate military court convicted her of spying and sentenced her—to be hanged by the neck until dead!

Born in New Orleans on June 10, 1833, she was the eldest daughter of eight offspring sired by a Spanish political refugee who had married a French woman before immigrating to the United States. When she was 10, her father moved the family to the frontier community of Grand Rapids, where he started a new career as an Indian trader. There, during the next eight years, she matured into a young lady endowed with "health, beauty and strong nerves."

Most of what we know of Pauline's early life comes from the biography penned by Philadelphia lawyer Ferdinand Sarmiento in 1865. However, certain elements of Sarmiento's biography, evidently written for Eastern readers used to thrilling dime novels, appear somewhat dubious.

There is the Leaping Thunder interlude, for example. He, a local Indian brave, fell in love with the beautiful Kent County teenager. To "the Laughing Breeze," as she

117

had been dubbed by Indian playmates, Leaping Thunder brought presents, finely wrought moccasins, fur garments and choice cuts of "buffalo hump." Owing to the distance lying between Grand Rapids and the nearest buffalo herd, the much esteemed hump must have been a bit gamy by the time of delivery.

Be that as it may, to further prove his manhood in Pauline's eyes, Leaping Thunder journeyed west to fight a fierce battle with rival tribesmen in a narrow mountain pass where he "made many of the foe bite the dust beneath his bow and lance." Chief Leaping Thunder returned to Grand Rapids to claim his well earned prize only to discover that the Laughing Breeze had blown out of town to parts unknown.

Eventually, 18-year-old Pauline wound up in New York City where she launched a stage career. When New York audiences failed to recognize her talent, she accepted an engagement at the New Orleans Varieties Theatre. Shortly thereafter, she married Charles Dickinson, a fellow actor, and she begat a large family.

But the Fates had in mind for Pauline a more dramatic role than that of happily married mother. All of her children died young, including four who were swept away by diphtheria in one day. When the Civil War broke out, Dickinson enlisted as a musician in the Union Army. He succumbed to dysentery in 1862.

Tragically bereft of her entire family, the comely widow returned to the stage. March of 1863 found her playing at a theatre in Louisville, Kentucky, where a pair of paroled Confederate officers offered her $300 to deliver a pro-Southern toast during a performance.

She immediately reported that offer to the local provost marshall. He suggested she make the toast and thereby launch a career sub rosa as a Union spy. Dressed as a "gentleman of fashion" in the role of Plutella in "The Seven Sisters," she raised a glass to the packed house and toasted: "Here's to Jeff Davis and the Southern Confederacy. May the South always maintain her honor and her rights!

The loyal and rebel factions in the audience responded with a "mingled storm of applause and condemnation," and Pauline was fired from the cast. Having thus established her reputation as a "virulent secessionist," the provost marshall commissioned her as a secret agent with instructions to penetrate as far south as possible and collect military information but to make no notes or maps.

At Shelbyville and Tullahoma, Tennessee, however, the temptation became too great. She rendered careful drawings of Confederate emplacements, which she secreted between the soles of her boots. Having those documents made her nervous, and when routinely question by a patrol, she panicked and galloped away into the night. After eluding her pursuers for several days, she was eventually captured, searched and the damaging documents were discovered.

Her captors took her to the dashing cavalry leader, Brig. Gen. John Hunt Morgan, who while reputedly swayed by her beauty, passed her on to Brig. Gen. Nathan Bedford Forrest. Despite the incriminating documents, even the fierce Forrest could not fully make up his mind about her guilt. He sent her to Bragg for further questioning.

Following his interrogation, Bragg had her incarcerated at Shelbyville while a military court pondered her case. Pauline sickened under the strain, and when the court sentenced her to the gallows 10 days later, she completely collapsed. The chivalrous Confederates delayed her hanging until they could nurse her back to health.

But before the sentence could be consummated, Bragg was forced to suddenly evacuate Shelbyville on June 27 before Maj. Gen. William S. Rosecrans' advancing army. Pauline was left behind. She delivered an intelligence report to the Union officers who liberated her, and that information proved of value to the Army of the Cumberland as it moved through Tennessee.

Her usefulness as a secret agent at an end, Pauline returned north to be lionized as a symbol of patriotism. President Lincoln commended her, and Maj. Gen. James A. Garfield proclaimed her an honorary major of cavalry. She returned to the stage wearing her major's uniform and "traveled far and wide" lecturing on her deeds. Her reputation as a spy was second only to her Confederate counterpart, Belle Boyd.

Alas, this high point of her life lasted but briefly. Inevitably, audiences wearied of the "lady spy of the Cumberland."

Following the war, she drifted westward, still performing in uniform and embellishing her exploits with each telling. Her career went rapidly downhill. She married a succession of ne'er-do-well Californians and became a drug addict. On December 2, 1893, she committed suicide by overdosing on morphine.

The San Francisco chapter of the Grand Army of the Republic escorted her flower-laden casket to the veterans' section of the city cemetery, a squad fired a volley over her grave, a bugler sounded taps and the perils of Pauline were ended.

When Michigan's David Battled a Confederate Goliath

Col. Orlando Moore.

In 1863, America had little cause to celebrate the anniversary of its birth. A struggle to determine whether the Union would survive had bloodied the nation for more than two years. On that Independence Day, the besieged citizens of Vicksburg, Mississippi, huddled in caves and ate mule meat if they were lucky, and burial details moved among the green farm fields of Gettysburg, littered with tangled piles of blue and gray.

Yet, it was the Fourth of July, the most patriotic of all American holidays. And no patriot remembered that fact with more fervor than Col. Orlando Moore from Schoolcraft, as he and 200 men of the 25th Michigan Infantry regiment, outnumbered 10 to 1 by an attacking Confederate cavalry force led by Gen. John Hunt Morgan, and with no hope of reinforcements, faced near-certain annihilation.

At dawn, Morgan had sent a couple of cannonballs crashing into their position, killing and maiming. Then he ordered a cease fire and sent forward a flag of truce. Moore rode out between the lines to meet the delegation of Confederate officers.

Col. R.A. Alston, Morgan's chief-of-staff, saluted Moore and handed him the following dispatch: "To the Officer Commanding the Federal Forces at Stockade near Green River Bridge, Kentucky: Sir,—In the name of the Confederate States government I demand an immediate and unconditional surrender of the entire force under your command, together with the stockade. I am, very respectfully, sir, John H. Morgan, Commanding Division Cav. C.S.A."

Moore smiled as he replied, "Present my compliments to General Morgan, and say to him that this being the Fourth of July I cannot entertain the proposition to surrender."

Alston pleaded with him to reconsider and thus save useless bloodshed. Moore simply answered, "I have a duty to perform to my country."

Moved by that response, Alston shook his hand and said, "Goodbye, Colonel Moore; God only knows which us may fall first."

Then the officers wheeled their mounts, galloped back to their respective lines and Morgan's artillery opened fire.

Born in Wilkesbarre, Pennsylvania, on July 13, 1827, as a youth Moore had immigrated with his parents to Schoolcraft. He later moved to Kalamazoo where he became a portrait painter. Among his subjects was Michigan Gov. Epaphroditus Ransom.

The stirring events of the 1850's that presaged the Civil War—the repeal of the Missouri Compromise and "bleeding Kansas"—aroused Moore's patriotism and he secured a second lieutenant's commission in the 6th U.S. Infantry in 1856. Stationed in California when the war broke out in April 1861, Moore requested to be transferred to the East.

He first served as lieutenant colonel of the 13th Michigan Infantry, which had been recruited in Kalamazoo. But when the 25th Michigan Infantry was organized in August 1862, he was commissioned its colonel.

For four weeks, Moore drilled the 10 companies of raw recruits from Berrien, Calhoun, Kalamazoo, Kent, Ionia, St. Joseph and Ottawa counties who gathered in Kalamazoo. Then on September 29, the 25th left for Louisville, proudly carrying a battle flag bearing the inscription, "This flag is given in faith that it will be carried where honor and duty lead," which had been presented by the citizens of Kalamazoo.

For nine months, the 25th performed routine scouting and guard duty in the area south of Louisville. But July 2, 1863, found Moore with only 200 of his normal strength of nearly 900 men stationed at a small fortress that guarded a bridge over the Green River, approximately 10 miles north of Columbia, Kentucky. That afternoon, he received a scouting report—Morgan's force of 3,000 to 4,000 cavalrymen had crossed the Cumberland River to invade Kentucky.

Despite his weak force, Moore determined not to retreat but to attempt to at least retard the progress of the Confederate raiders. He rode out to scout the surrounding country

123

and discovered an ideal site to make a stand, on the south side of the river about two miles from his base. there, the road from Columbia to Lebanon ran through a peninsula formed by a horseshoe bend of the Green River. An open five-acre field was bordered by the steep riverbank on the north and deep ravines on the south.

Moore's men constructed earthworks in the middle of the field, within musket fire of the closest point the Confederates could plant a cannon. A strong force, however, could easily capture that small fortification. But Moore was playing a game of chess with Morgan, and the fortification in the open was the pawn.

While 75 of his men raised the earthworks, the remainder chopped down trees in the woods to the rear and on each side of the field to form an abatis to stop a cavalry charge and behind which his men could take cover.

Following Moore's refusal to surrender, Morgan's artillery opened up on the Michigan position. Moore's first order to the 25 men in the earthworks was "rise up and pick those gunners at the battery." Having grown up among the woods of southern Michigan, where hunting was a way of life, the infantrymen were excellent marksmen. Those cannoners that were not dropped by the deadly volley of musket fire soon broke and ran, leaving the artillery pieces behind.

Then, just as Moore had planned, a brigade of Confederate cavalrymen charged the earthworks on foot. As the Michigan men had been instructed, they evacuated the fortification, running to the woods on either side. When the Confederates leaped over the earthen banks, they found themselves directly exposed to the fire of the Michigan sharpshooters hidden among the fallen trees to the rear.

With hideous rebel yells, they charged the Michigan front, but they could not withstand the murderous firepower. Eight times the Confederates charged, and eight times they were driven back.

Meanwhile, another of Morgan's regiments had been

cutting its way through the fallen trees bordering the field. It opened fire on the Michigan right flank. Moore had held in reserve Company I, made up of Dutch immigrants from Holland, Michigan. While Moore blew the bugle, giving the impression that a large relief force was advancing, the Hollanders fired on the rebels with such deadly accuracy that they retreated.

For 3 1/2 hours, the battle raged. Then, amazingly, Morgan retreated. He had lost 50 men killed, including some of his finest officers, and 200 wounded. Moore's casualties were 6 dead and 22 wounded. Morgan succeeded in crossing the river at another point, but the 12 hours he lost in doing so caused him to abandon his plan to sack Louisville.

Despite the drubbing he received, Morgan could not help but admire his adversary's skillful tactics. He reportedly remarked that Morgan should be promoted to brigadier general.

That, however, never happened. It seems Moore had the habit of criticizing inept superiors. Moore survived the war, remained in the army and fought Indians out West. He retired as a lieutenant colonel in 1884.

And of all his many battles, none was more glorious than when the Union David defeated the Confederate Goliath on July 4, 1863.

Escape from Libby Prison

Lt. James M. Wells from Schoolcraft.

L t. James M. Wells of the 8th Michigan Cavalry grunted and squirmed his way along the narrow tunnel that had been painstakingly burrowed over a seven-week period. It extended eight feet beneath a side street in Richmond, Virginia. Behind, lay a little-used room the soldiers called "rat hell" in the basement of the infamous Libby Prison. Ahead, lay possible release from near-starvation and brutal treatment.

Gasping for breath in the 16-inch-diameter tunnel, Wells succeeded in dragging himself its 50-foot length. He suddenly clawed through a hole in the floor of a vacant shed across the street from the prison. Sucking in great drafts of the first fresh air he had tasted in six months, Wells knew the most hazardous part of his bid for freedom awaited him.

The 27-year-old cavalryman was no stranger to adventure. Born in 1837 in western New York, Wells immigrated with his family to Kalamazoo County in the early 1840's. His father, Samuel D. Wells, acquired a 40-acre homestead in Comstock Township, where young Wells experienced a typical frontier childhood. Wells was a teenager when his father died and his mother moved the family to the village of Schoolcraft.

Wells attended Kalamazoo College for a while, but in 1857, in company with Clem Stone, the eldest son of the college president, James A. B. Stone, he left for the "Mormon War." U.S. troops had been dispatched to Utah Territory to put down an alleged rebellion by Brigham Young and his followers.

Wells signed on as a "bull-whacker" to drive one of the hundreds of ox-drawn supply wagons that were part of the expedition. The bloodless war ended in a compromise the following year. In the meantime, Wells had quit to go on a thrilling trip down the Missouri River. He next knocked around the Southern frontier for a spell before returning to Schoolcraft.

There, in December 1862, the 25-year-old enlisted as a

127

first sergeant in Company F, 8th Michigan Cavalry. Wells' older brother John and his four cousins also enlisted in various units. Thirteen-year-old cousin Elmer served as a drummer boy in the 25th Michigan Infantry.

Wells' first assignment led him to Detroit, where he guarded barracks filled with conscripts who had been paid a bounty to serve in someone else's place. Those men required guarding until they could be shipped to the front because of their notorious tendency to desert with the bounty money and then repeat the lucrative feat elsewhere under an alias.

The men of Wells' company elected him second lieutenant on March 2, 1863, and shortly thereafter, the 8th Michigan Cavalry was ordered to eastern Kentucky. There, under command of Col. Elisha Mix of Allegan, it hunted guerrilla bands and Confederate raiders.

The 8th Michigan spent most of the month of July, 1863, in pursuit of Brig. Gen. John Hunt Morgan as he staged a spectacular 700-mile raid through Ohio. Wells participated in the Battle of Buffington's Island, which turned the tide against Morgan. Approximately 2,300 of the Confederate raiders were captured there, but their wily general managed to slip through the federal lines. The 8th Michigan finally caught up with Morgan at New Lisbon where he surrendered.

In August, the 8th Michigan marched from Kentucky to participate in the East Tennessee Campaign. Then, on September 26, 1863, the brigade they were attached to was attacked by Brig. Gen. Nathan Bedford Forrest's command of 15,000 soldiers. The inferior Union force fought bravely, then broke and ran. Wells retreated on a stray horse and took refuge for the night in a civilian household. He awoke to find a Confederate cavalryman with gun in hand standing over him.

Transported by rail via Atlanta, Wells arrived at Libby Prison a month later. A three-story, 110-by-140-foot warehouse, formerly the property of Libby & Son Ship Chandlers & Grocers, it had been converted for incarceration of Union officers. While not as gruesome as the major stockade for enlisted men at Andersonville, Georgia, life at Libby was bad enough.

Approximately 1,200 officers were packed into the top floor of the structure. They slept without blankets on hardwood floors and survived on scant rations they cooked themselves. Wells recalled getting up in the night to scrape and eat the burned rice from the bottom of kettles that had been left to soak. Nevertheless, the prisoners maintained good discipline and kept their quarters spotlessly clean.

The men devised endless escape plans, but most proved impractical. One well-laid plan that would have resulted in the mass escape of all the prisoners held in the Confederate capital, some 15,000-20,000 men, failed because a traitor revealed the secret. As a result, the tunneling attempt was made known to only 200 hand-picked officers.

The men were able to work their way down to the little-used basement room, known as "rat-hell" because it was the lair of the big rodents, by breaking a passage down through the rear of the fireplaces. After lights out each night, two men slipped down to the basement while others kept watch. Using clam shells and table knives, the men slowly burrowed beneath the street. The dirt removed was scattered on the floor and covered with straw. Each morning, the rear of the fireplace was rebricked and carefully camouflaged with soot.

When the tunnelers calculated they had reached their goal, they made an exploratory hole upwards. The knife blade came up in the road a few paces from a sentry. Fortunately, they were able to stop up the hole without being detected and continue the tunnel forward.

Finally, on the night of February 9, 1864, after more than seven weeks of work, all was in readiness. One-by-one, Wells and 108 of his comrades slithered through the tunnel. A sentinel paced his post within 10 feet of the shed, so the men each waited for him to do an about-face and walk away before they singly slipped into the night. Some managed to link up with companions, but Wells was by himself.

He made it out of the city and waded the shallow Chickahoming River. Hiding by day, he stumbled for the next six nights through dense lowlands toward the Union positions at Williamsburg. Nearly dead form exposure and starvation, he was picked up by a federal cavalry patrol. Of the 109 men who escaped Libby Prison, 48 were recaptured.

Wells went home to Michigan on a 30-day furlough and then returned to combat duty with the rank of captain. In late July 1864, he participated in Maj. Gen. George Stoneman's raid intended to release the more than 30,000 Union prisoners held at Macon and Andersonville. But Maj. Gen. Joseph Wheeler's cavalry routed the Union force and captured Stoneman and 700 of his men near Macon.

Once again, Wells was an unwilling guest of the Confederacy. He languished in Camp Oglethorpe, near Macon, along with many former Libby prisoners who had been moved further south, until on September 28, 1864, he was exchanged for six Confederate prisoners.

Wells served as a cavalry officer until the war's end, participating in the Franklin and Nashville, Tennessee, campaigns and in fighting guerrillas in Tennessee. He was discharged on July 20, 1865.

Wells recounted his Civil war exploits in his autobiography, *With Touch of Elbow,* published in 1909. Libby Prison was dismantled in 1889 and reconstructed in Chicago as a museum.

The Rise and Fall of Michigan's Bloomers

Sister Ellen G. White's version of the bloomer-ensemble set Battle Creek tongues wagging.

It is immodest apparel, wholly unfitted for the modest, humble followers of Christ," wrote Sister Ellen G. White in 1864. White, in concert with husband James and a coterie of church elders, had labored long and hard to bring respectability to her Battle Creek-based sect, the Seventh Day Adventist Church. Now, some of her wayward followers were heaping ridicule upon themselves and the church by parading around the streets of Battle Creek in the pants and skirt ensemble known as "bloomers."

Sister White might have lapsed into vision, as she frequently did to set church dogma. But that strenuous effort was not necessary in this case. She had merely to quote scripture—Deuteronomy 22:5: "The woman shall not wear that which pertaineth unto a man, neither shall a man put on a woman's garment: for all that do so are abomination unto the Lord thy God."

This sartorial tempest in a teapot had scandalized the nation beginning in the 1840s. True, in the 1820s, the lady colonists at Robert Owen's utopian community at New Harmony, Indiana, had experimented with a knee-length tunic worn over baggy trousers gathered at the ankle, a la harem. But they had kept pretty much to themselves in the Hoosier hinterland.

It was when feminist Elizabeth Smith Miller began wearing a similar outfit in polite society that jaws began dropping. Other audacious femmes, including Elizabeth Cady Stanton, Susan B. Anthony and the Grimke sisters, also garbed themselves in what became known as the "reform dress." In contrast to the customary apparel of the period—dresses so long that women needed to lift them while walking and ponderous hoop-skirts—the reform dress offered a freedom of movement as well as a symbol of emancipation from the fetters of a male-dominated society.

Amelia Bloomer championed the reform dress in her journal, *The Lily,* the first periodical "owned, edited and controlled by a woman and published in the interests of women." As a result, her name became synonymous with the avant-garde style as well as those who wore it.

But most American men, it seems, had set their minds on wearing the only pants in the family. Everywhere, the bloomers were met with derision. Mrs. M.M. Jones, who had adopted the style, complained., "however modestly you may pass about your business, base rowdies congregated around street corners, hotel steps and lager beer saloons will look at you in a manner that will cause every drop of blood to run cold within you veins. Children, hooting and shouting and yelling, today pelt you with snowballs, and tomorrow with apple cores."

Jones gave up her comfortable outfit as did most of the other women's rights activists within a few years. Amelia Bloomer held out for about eight years, then she too returned to the hoop and bustle.

In the meantime, however, bloomers had made their appearance in Michigan. During the early 1850's, James Jesse Strang, king of the Mormon colony on Beaver Island, had decreed bloomers to be the national costume for his female subjects, including the four women he had taken as his wives. Polygamy was one thing, but to force their wives to wear the "immodest" garb seemed a bit extreme to several of Strang's followers. But those who refused faced a public flogging.

Bloomers, in fact, may have led to Strang's demise. Thomas Bedford, who had been lashed for defying the bloomer law, was one of the two Mormons who assassinated their king in 1856

By the early 1860's, the flap about dress reform had largely subsided as the nation turned its energies to the Civil War. The Adventist ladies were late bloomers, so to speak. To complicate matters, Battle Creek was also a Midwestern stronghold of the Spiritualists. Along with seances and ouija boards, many Spiritualist ladies had also embraced the bloomer outfit. Sister White, who hated that rival sect with a righteous passion, learned to her chagrin

133

that Battle Creek townsfolk were confusing those among her flock who wore bloomers with the local "rappers."

Strangely enough, however, following a visit to Dr. James Caleb Jackson's hydropathic spa in Dansville, New York, White suddenly reversed her stand on bloomers. Jackson, from who White also borrowed the concept of the hydropathic clinic that would evolve into the Battle Creek Sanitarium, had long advocated bloomers for health reasons.

In any event, White penned a "Testimony for the Church" in1867 in which she recommended the adoption of a "reform short dress." To those who found contradiction in her variant visions she testily chided, "I must contend that I am the best judge of the things that have been presented before me in vision; and none need fear that I shall by my life contradict my own testimony..."

White's version of the bloomer ensemble featured a plain dress "short enough to clear the filth of the sidewalk and street, without being raised by the hand." In other words, "the dress should reach somewhat below the top of the boot." Misinterpreting her words, some naughty Adventists began hemming their dresses just below the knees at a level with men's boots. Those mini-bloomers, she scolded in no uncertain terms, were way too high for decency. "Nine inches from the ground" and no shorter, she stipulated in a later testimony.

In order to head off any such future risque deviations, White, who was also not above making a buck, merchandised "approved" reform dress patterns at $1, postpaid. She herself donned bloomers for walks around town and while preaching from the local pulpit. So as not to shock other audiences, however, she maintained a more decorous wardrobe for travels away from Battle Creek.

Alas, neither her countrymen nor the bulk of her followers were yet ready for bloomers. As the controversy continued, White quietly returned to less ostentatious apparel. Not until the 1890's, when women participated in the

national mania for bicycling, would bloomers again defy
the nation's morals.

The Philo Parsons Affair

The U.S.S. Michigan.

The big side-wheel paddles of the Philo Parsons lashed the waters of the Detroit River white as it swung out from its dock near the foot of Woodward Avenue on the morning of September 19, 1864. On a routine run to Sandusky, Ohio, its fancy salon was packed with travelers, mainly women chatting with each other about the latest news from far-off Southern battlefields.

Little could anyone aboard the 135-foot steamer built in in Algonac in1861 have suspected that before the day was over they would be involved in one of the most bizarre episodes of the Civil War—a daring raid by Confederate sailors to capture a U.S. Navy gunboat, free thousands of Confederate prisoners held on Johnson Island, near Cedar Point, Ohio, and then attack Detroit and other Great Lakes cities.

The mastermind behind this plot to carry the war to the unsuspecting lake states and hopefully weaken the North's determination to continue the conflict was John Yates Beall, a slender 28-year-old Virginian, veteran of Stonewall Jackson's brigade and a commissioned Confederate privateer. He had first conceived the plan in 1862 while lying in a hospital bed recovering from a near-fatal battle wound.

The key to the venture lay in taking the USS Michigan. Launched at Erie, Pennsylvania, in 1844, the 600-ton, 168-foot side-wheel steamer was the Navy's first iron-hull vessel and the only American ship of war on the Great Lakes. It spent much of the war stationed off Johnson Island.

Not daring to risk antagonizing Great Britain should the raid involve Canada, Confederate Secretary of the Navy, Stephen R. Mallory, shelved the plan in 1862. But two years later, facing depleted resources and manpower and with the growing despair following the fall of Atlanta, Mallory gave his approval for Beall to make the attempt.

Other key participants joining Beall in the conspiracy included Jacob Thompson, who directed a spy and sabotage ring from Windsor, Canada; his trusted aide, Godfrey

137

J. Hyams of Little Rock, Arkansas; Capt. Charles H. Cole, who had ridden with Confederate Cavalry leader John Hunt Morgan; and Bennet G. Burleigh, a huge Scottish soldier of fortune.

Posing as a rich young Philadelphia lawyer, Cole set up his headquarters in Sandusky, where he soon managed to befriend Capt. Jack C. Carter, commanding officer of the Michigan. Carefully nurturing that friendship through lavish gifts of wine and cigars, Cole succeeded in getting invited several times to tour the gun boat. His role was to supply drugged champagne to the officers and men of the Michigan on the night of September 19 and announce his success to the waiting boarding party with a rocket signal.

Having captured the vessel, the raiders would turn its cannons on the prison on Johnson Island to support the escape of the 3,000 Confederate soldiers there. Equipped with arms supplied by secret friends of the Confederacy, the escaped prisoners would slash south through Ohio while the Michigan bombarded Detroit, Buffalo and other lake ports, thus spreading panic throughout the North.

Initially, the plot went well. Beall recruited 28 seamen, furnishing each with a Navy Colt revolver, ammunition and money. Burleigh booked passage on the Philo Parsons, requesting its captain to make a special stop at Sandwich, Canada, to pick up some friends.

Steaming out of Detroit at 8 a.m., the ship picked up Beall and two other young gentlemen at Sandwich and proceeded to its next scheduled stop at Amherstburg, Canada. There, a crowd of "roughly dressed men" carrying an old trunk stomped up the gangplank. About 4 p.m., after the vessel had left Kelly Island, the raiders made their move.

Opening the trunk and passing out revolvers, hatchets and knives, the privateers herded the frightened passengers into the main cabin. Leveling his pistol at the captain's head, Beall announced: "I am a Confederate officer. There are 30 of us, well armed. I seize this boat and take you as prisoner." The Philo Parsons had just joined the

Confederate Navy.

Since it was too early to approach the Michigan and the ship was running low on fuel, Beall had the vessel steam back to Bass Island to take on wood. There, another passenger steamer, the Island Queen, docked next to the Philo Parsons. The raiders streamed over its side and took all its passengers, including 35 unarmed soldiers from Ohio, prisoner.

Placing the soldiers "on parole" and forcing the other passengers from both vessels to swear they would keep silent about the raid for 24 hours, Beall put them ashore. He then towed the Island Queen three miles out and scuttled it. It drifted away, sinking on a nearby reef in nine feet of water.

Reaching Sandusky Harbor after nightfall, Beall cast anchor and awaited the signal from the Michigan. That signal was never to come. Thanks to detailed intelligence reports from Hyams, a double agent, Col. Bennett H. Hill in charge of the Detroit district, had been closely monitoring the conspiracy almost from its inception. Hill had wired Carter of the Michigan about Cole's duplicity. Carter's men had burst into Cole's Sandusky hotel room and arrested him as a spy.

After waiting several hours for the signal, Beall decided to make the attempt anyway. But his men refused to risk their lives in such a foolhardy manner. When the crew signed a memorandum admitting that it was they who had backed out, Beall turned the vessel around and steamed toward Detroit. Raising the "Stars and Bars," the Philo Parsons, however, took the precaution to hug the Canadian shore. At Sandwich, her main feed pipe was opened, and as the hull began to settle in the water, the raiders clambered over her sides to escape into Canada.

News of the Confederate pirate raid spread quickly to Detroit and other lake ports, throwing citizens into a temporary panic. When the initial excitement died down, however, the raid ultimately had the opposite effect from

139

what the Confederates had desired. Angry Midwesterners intensified their zeal to prosecute the war.

The USS Michigan remained in service until 1928. The Philo Parsons was towed to port before it sank and was soon again plying the waters of Lake Erie. The Island Queen also was salvaged, none the worst for its sinking. Most of the raiders succeeded in getting back behind Southern lines. Beall and Burleigh, however, remained in Canada to conduct further mischief. Ultimately, both were captured.

Burleigh escaped during his trial and made his way back to Scotland where he went on to carve out a noted career as a military journalist. Cole remained a prisoner until 1866 when he was released on a writ of habeas corpus.

Not so fortunate was Beall. Despite his protests that he was entitled to be treated as a regular prisoner of war, he was court-martialed, convicted as a spy and guerrilla and hanged on February 4, 1865.

Fayette: Boom Town to Ghost Town

An 1873 Lithograph of Fayette.

A shower of sparks sizzled through the air when the ironworker knocked out the clay plug at the mouth of the huge blast furnace. Then came a lava-like stream of impurities that would congeal into cinders and slag. Finally, the white-hot molten iron sputtered and steamed through channels in a bed of sand, an intricate system of molds that resembled rows of piglets suckling a sow. Hours later, the fiery liquid would harden into 150-pound bars appropriately called "pig iron."

From 1867 through 1890, such scenes were a common occurrence at Fayette, a community of 500 residents located on the west coast of the Garden Peninsula approximately 20 miles due east of Escanaba. Yet, the tapping of the blast furnaces there rarely failed to attract spectators who marveled at the pyrotechnics. Among the knot of tourists who observed such a scene in the summer of 1869 was the Rev. James Hibbert Langille.

Langille had journeyed to the north country to vacation with his friend and relative, Dr. Seth Sloan, who, as proprietor of the Jackson Iron Company store at Fayette, dispensed "pills, pork, castor oil and calicoes among his customers with the utmost impartiality." Langille found the local scenery spectacular. Opposite the New England-type village planted on a tiny peninsula that curled into Big Bay De Noc, limestone cliffs rose 150 feet from the shores of Snail Shell Harbor.

Langille had taken great exhilarating gulps of the cool, pine-laden air while pulling bass from the transparent waters of the harbor. Yet, he had also witnessed things that made his heart heavy. The Irish and French Canadian ironworkers had delivered "a volley of oaths that was perfectly terrible" when sparks from the furnace landed on them. He had felt his "very blood chill" at the curses uttered when others cut their hands while handling the sharp-edged pig iron. There was no church in Fayette, and, although the Jackson Iron Company had banned liquor from the village, the workers frequently spreed at the floating grog shops

142

that anchored offshore and at the blind pigs located farther down the beach. In short, Langille had found "a place given over to worldly good, while God was wholly forgotten."

Langille recorded his campaign to start a Sunday school in the tough community, hoping the "sheep would follow the lambs," in the form of a juvenile novel, *Snail Shell Harbor,* published in Boston in 1870. While poor of plot, weak in characterization and excessively moralistic in tone, the volume is invaluable as a historical source because it contains practically the only surviving descriptions of life at Fayette in the early days.

The genesis of Fayette took place as a result of the completion of the Peninsula Railroad, linking Negaunee with Escanaba, in 1864. A 1,300-foot-long ore dock constructed at Escanaba made it possible for the Jackson Iron Company to ship ore from its rich mines at Negaunee by rail and hence by ship to Cleveland. But transporting the bulky ore over that long haul cut deep into profits. Furthermore, when winter's ice ended the shipping season, the ore had to be stockpiled.

Fayette Brown, manager of the Jackson Iron Company, sought to relieve that bottleneck through the establishment of a company-owned iron furnace. A survey expedition conducted in 1864 had located an ideal site at Snail Shell Harbor. The harbor was deep enough to accommodate heavy shipping. The limestone deposits offered an accessible supply of lime used to remove impurities from the iron. Most importantly, the peninsula was blanketed by a heavy growth of hardwood that could be converted into charcoal.

By 1867, the company had acquired 16,000 acres of prime timberland surrounding the site, which was named Fayette in honor of its manager. That May, workmen began building a 46-foot-high furnace made of limestone blocks quarried from the nearby cliffs. Christmas Day of the year saw the first smelting of pig iron.

By Langille's visit in 1869, Fayette had become quite a

boom town. Company officials resided in fashionable New England-style "salt box" homes, while the 200 mill employees and their families lived in log cabins clustered around the harbor. A company store, office building, carpenter shop, blacksmith shop, barn and other structures provided for the various needs of man and beast. Later amenities included an opera house, race track and church.

Company employees plied specialized tasks. Some were involved in the production of charcoal. Hardwood cut into four-foot lengths was either converted to charcoal at several pits located in the woods or transported by ship or narrow gauge railroad to the main charcoal kilns at Fayette. Those were igloo-shaped stone structures 25 feet in diameter. Filled with forty cords of green hardwood and dry kindling, the kilns were sealed off to allow a slow charring of the contents. Following several days of controlled burning, the charcoal was shoveled out into scuttle baskets and conveyed to the furnace.

A tugboat pulled scows of iron ore from Escanaba to Fayette, where it was finely crushed by power machinery. Another specialized kiln baked limestone into lime. Steam-powered hoists lifted a precisely proportioned charge of ore, lime, clay and charcoal to hoppers that were dumped into the top of the furnace. A second furnace was added in 1870, and the ruddy glow of the great fires that lit up the evening sky became a familiar sight at Fayette.

By 1875, Fayette' annual production of pig iron had reached 14,075 tons. Ultimately, 229,288 tons of iron were produced there. But the enormous amount of charcoal consumed in the furnaces eventually spelled doom for the community. An acre yielded an average of four cords of hardwood. A cord of wood could be converted to about 50 bushels of charcoal, and it took twice that to produce a ton of iron.

By 1890, the surrounding countryside had been denuded of timber. The mill closed down, and most of the machinery was dismantled and moved to other sites. The town's population followed likewise, and Fayette became a ghost town.

In 1916, the Cleveland Cliffs Iron Co., which acquired the town once valued at $300,000, sold it for a pittance to two men from Ashland, Wisconsin. Nature took its toll over the years, waves pounded the dock to pieces, the charcoal kilns collapsed and many of the other structures lay in ruin.

In 1959, the Michigan Department of Conservation, forerunner of the Department of Natural Resources, acquired Fayette and 171 surrounding acres as a state park. Adjacent acreage was added over the following two decades, and the DNR, in conjunction with the Michigan History Division of the Department of State, restored some structures, added an interpretive center and converted Fayette into a living history exhibit.

The ghost town of Fayette is now one of Michigan's most picturesque historic sites.

The Love Lives of a Head Master

Dr. Thomas Sheldon Andrews,
the match-making phrenologist, in 1879.

Dr. Thomas Sheldon Andrews, the celebrated match-making phrenologist, frowned as he fingered the head of "the tall, comely lady" who had taken the seat on stage. She was going to be a tough case to "pair off" with someone else in the audience.

Phrenology, the science of ascertaining character by the shape of the head and facial features and, in particular, through the analysis of a series of bumps on the skull, enabled Andrews to predict the compatibility of couples. Phrenologists had carefully mapped out the human skull into 34 zones, each responsible for such traits as combativeness, spirituality, self-esteem, etc. None was more significant in this case than the "organ of amativeness," the Victorian euphemism for love, situated to the back of the head slightly below the ears.

Still feeling the lady's bumps, Andrews scanned the sea of strangers before him, searching for just the right combination of brow, eyebrow and jaw. Suddenly, he stopped and, pointing to a man in the back row by the door, called him forward to the stage. When he took the chair next to the comely lady, the audience roared. Andrews had picked the lady's very husband, who, returning from a trip, had slipped into the audience late—and they were "good mates" to be sure.

Andrews, one of scores of itinerant phrenologists who advised, cured, mated and otherwise bamboozled their 19th century countrymen, had come upon his knowledge of bumps the hard way—that is, via the school of hard knocks. Born in 1829 in an inn managed by his parents on the Royal Oak and Pontiac Turnpike near Detroit, he had ample opportunity while growing up there and in Pontiac, where the family moved in 1841, to observe the effects of a poorly matched couple—his parents.

His mother, Ann, as Andrews later analyzed, had been endowed with an excess of the traits of conscientiousness and will. Moreover, she had "large facial features and a Washington (President George, that is) cast of countenance." In short, her phrenological development was that of a leader.

On the other hand, his father Ira's "combativeness and destructiveness were prominent and acute," particularly when he was under the influence of alcohol. Frequently driven to drink by the realization that his wife was his better, he would return home in his cups to argue. While his wife sometimes argued back, her usual response was to ignore him and sing Methodist hymns in a loud voice, which irritated him all the more.

At the age of 17, Andrews left his quarrelsome parents, shipping on as a cabin boy aboard the passenger steamboat "Constellation," which plied the Detroit to Buffalo run. He stayed on the lakes over the next seven years, eventually working his way up to the coveted position of caterer and steward.

In the meantime, when 19 years old, he became infatuated with a beautiful young acquaintance and rushed into marriage with her before, evidently, he had given her head a good going over. He soon discovered to his dismay that, like himself, she was "high spirited and headstrong." Furthermore, he later learned from her father that "he had never been able to subdue her will."

During the ensuing five years, when the Andrews were not battling over who was to wear the pants in the family, they succeeded in producing two offspring. In 1853, Andrews left the life of a sailor to become a hotel proprietor in Eagle River in the remote Keweenaw Peninsula.

Things went well for his new endeavor but not for his family life. Remarking that she "would never bear any more children," his wife suddenly quit their marriage bed. Two weeks later, without so much as a "howdy do," she had her trunks loaded on a departing steamer and left him and the children for parts unknown.

A year later, Andrews tracked her down and they had a brief reconciliation, but then she "pulled away for good." He secured a divorce in 1857. What really hurt, however,

148

and underscored that their wrecked marriage was the result of incompatible bumps, was that Andrews learned she soon remarried and happily bore her new spouse six children.

Grief-stricken but none the wiser, a few months later, Andrews rushed impetuously into another marriage with a young Detroit schoolteacher, the daughter of a Presbyterian minister. Alas, this too was a mismatch. While Andrews preferred quiet nights at home poring over the latest issue of the *Phrenological Journal* or atlases of the cranium, his new wife gadded about town, socializing and shopping. Their bumpy marriage lasted little more than a year.

Heartbroken once again, Andrews immersed himself in his phrenological studies. He had the supreme honor of having his own head done by the master of them all, Prof. Orson S. Fowler, in Chicago in 1865. Based on that examination, the professor told him: "You must marry a woman full-chested and full-cheeked, round-favored, features regular, forehead full in the middle and lower portions..."

Andrews took the professor's advice to heart. He bypassed many a pretty face that did not quite fit the phrenological bill. Once, a rich man who had befriended him offered Andrews $1,000 and a new team and carriage to marry his attractive niece. Andrews took one look at the back of her head and promptly left town.

Then, oh glorious day, he found his soul mate, Annie. It was love at first sight. True, the engraving of her he inserted in his 1879 autobiography depicted a walking hogshead of a matron with scowling countenance little likely to attract many other suitors. But then they did not know her head as Andrews did. He found her leading phrenological developments to be: perception, order, comparison, language, hope, benevolence, veneration, conscientiousness, firmness, spirituality and, oh yes, amativeness. Those meshed with his own bumps like a marriage made in heaven.

What is more, Annie, too, firmly believed in phrenology. Soon, Dr. & Mrs. Dr. Andrews took to the road to deliver their double-barreled head lectures to audiences across the land, thus spreading the marital wisdom the Andrews had grown to fervently believe: "If at first you don't succeed, try, try again," or there's more to love than looks—the right bumps help, too.

Mrs. "Dr." Annie Andrews, her bumps were perfect.

Joseph Coveney's Freethinker's Monument

Joseph Coveney, Buchanan's freethinker.

C areful not to tread on anyone's grave out of respect for the dead, the man moved purposefully through Oak Ridge Cemetery in the Berrien County village of Buchanan. He was proud of his slight limp, a souvenir of the late Rebellion; of the GAR button on his lapel; that he was a Republican, a Mason and a Protestant churchgoer, traits essential for a community leader in Michigan of 1874.

In an era when shiny brass spittoons occupied a prominent spot in all public places, even the hallowed halls of Congress, his right jaw bulged with a big quid of "eatin' tobacco." He walked up to the most prominent monument in the cemetery, furrowed his brow and let fly with a stream of brown fluid. It splattered against the tombstone chest high and cascaded down its elaborately chiseled side. Pausing a bit to admire the effects of his handiwork, he mumbled "damned atheist" and ambled away.

Who the expectorator was no one in Buchanan knew for sure, or at least they were not telling. Nor was he the only one to desecrate the monument erected in 1874. Others battered off chunks of the stone, attempted to mask the inscriptions with red chalk and, as local legend has it, Sunday school teachers led their classes to the site armed with sandpaper.

Throughout Berrien County, ministers thundered from the pulpit against the tombstone, newspapers carried debates on the "monumental question" and sidewalk loungers talked of little else that season. In short, the "freethinker's monument" had stirred up a hornet's nest of public opinion. And that suited Joseph Coveney just fine.

Born in County Cork, Ireland, March 29, 1805, Coveney left school at the age of 13 to become a weaver. When he was 21, he immigrated to America. He stayed in New York City for four years, where he learned the carpenter's trade. Coveney continued to ply that craft when he moved west, first to Schuylkill County, Pennsylvania, then to the vicinity of South Bend, Indiana, in 1833.

Three years later, at the height of the Michigan land rush, Coveney rode up to Kalamazoo, the site of the Federal Land Office, and purchased a 40-acre tract in Buchanan Township at the going price for government land, $1.25 an acre. In 1837, he carried his new wife Louisa across the threshold of the log cabin he had built on his homestead. Coveney prospered as a farmer, and he gradually expanded his holdings until his farm had grown to 600 acres of prime wheat land. In 1849, he caught the gold fever and, in company with two other "49ers," journeyed by ox team to California. He returned by sailing ship a year later, his California adventure having been "not an unprofitable one financially."

Coveney was industrious and economical. His neighbors respected him as "a shrewd businessman, a good, practical farmer and an intelligent citizen." They also remembered his generosity in helping those down on their luck.

Yet, Coveney did not quite fit the mold in one important aspect—he was a freethinker in terms of religion. Whether memories of his native Ireland, that had been wracked by religious civil war for centuries; life among the "godless miners" out west; or a combination of factors caused him to hate the traditional Christian faith is uncertain. Perhaps he fell under the sway of Voltaire, Thomas Paine or some other apostle of freethinking.

One thing is certain. Having formulated his unconventional philosophy, Coveney was not about to keep it to himself. He delighted in debate and never hesitated "to express his views at any place or time." As if that were not enough to make him persona non grata in the conservative community, he named his horses "Jesus" and "Christ."

There is evidence to suggest that Coveney's own family, which ultimately numbered 13 children, did not uniformly embrace his anti-religious sentiments. His son William, for example, was married in the local Methodist parsonage in February 1873. Four months later, when Coveney's 13-

year-old daughter died, a memorial poem expressing religious sentiments that had been written by a family member appeared in the Buchanan newspaper.

Perhaps those actions by Coveney's family lulled the community into believing that the old freethinker had mellowed, when, in early 1874, he announced he intended to erect a $3,000 burial monument in Oak Ridge Cemetery. It was touted as "the finest piece of work of the kind anywhere in all this region of the country."

In February, the village council debated replatting the veterans section located at the front of the cemetery so the Coveney monument might be in a more conspicuous location, but the motion was defeated. Throughout the spring and summer, area newspapers kept the public well informed on the progress of the grand monument taking shape at Siewertsen & Schulte's Niles Marble Works.

Then, in September 1874, came the gala unveiling of the marble masterpiece. It was indeed grand; from a six-foot-square base, a marble shaft rose 16 feet in height. Engraved on its sides were many lines of text. It was when the folks started reading those lines that the community gasped in horror.

Coveney, it seems, had decided to use the monument as a forum for his unorthodox philosophy. Emblazoned in marble were such sentiments as "The more saints the more hypocrites," "The more religion the more lying," "God in the constitution is the end of liberty" and "Nature is the true God." Even more shocking to Victorian sensibilities was the statement "Thirty-two thousand virgins given by command of God to an army of twelve thousand to debauch," a reference to Moses' orders as described in Numbers, chapter 31.

Incensed Buchananites dashed off fiery letters that were printed in the local newspaper. In particular, one, D. Fisk, sometime justice of the peace and school inspector, championed the anti-monument cause. "Covered over with words of moral filth, falsehoods and obscene blasphemy," wrote Fisk, the monument was not fit to stand in the same cemetery where Christians were buried. Coveney would be lucky if citizens did not "tear the lying thing down and sink it in eternal oblivion in the nearest frog pond at hand" or if the God of the Bible did not "hurl a thunderbolt at the blasphemous thing and shiver it into shapeless atoms."

Protagonists waged a holy war of words in the newspaper throughout the remainder of the year. Some used more than words and hacked at, spit on and tried to grind off the offending words. But, in testimony to the tolerance of the Buchanan community in a less tolerant age than today's, the monument survived.

Coveney purchased a full page biography of himself that was published in *The History of Berrien and VanBuren Counties* in 1880. His and Louisa's likenesses graced the top of the page. As sometimes happens when man and wife spend many years pulling together in harness, their visages had grown to resemble "two peas in a pod." The author of the biography quoted Coveney as believing a local minister's son had defaced his tombstone. The writer also noted that the monument was "an ornament to the cemetery, although at close view the stain of tobacco juice mars its beauty."

Coveney died, an unrepentant freethinker, in 1897. He was buried at the foot of his beloved monument, which still stands in Oak Ridge Cemetery, although the ravages of time, to say nothing of sandpaper, have nearly obliterated portions of the chiseled inscriptions.

When Pig-Boats Rode the Waves

Whalebacks preparing to lock through the Sault Canal, ca. 1900.

Hands blistered raw and arms bone-weary, Capt. Alexander McDougall rowed on. He was, you see, a stubborn Scot.

Unable to ply his normal trade of Great Lake's cargo ship captain because of a depression that had hit in 1873, McDougall had decided to investigate reports of coal deposits along the southern shore of Lake Superior. So one day in 1875, he loaded a rented dinghy aboard the steamer Winslow at the Sault. Lowered from the vessel several miles off the mouth of the Two Hearted River, McDougall rowed to shore.

Had he been looking for agates he might have had better luck, but a day's exploration along that rocky coast yielded no sign of coal. That evening McDougall rowed out to catch a passing steamer, but the ship failed to see his signal. With a stiff wind blowing offshore, the plucky Scot was forced to row some 25 miles east before he could beach his little craft at Whitefish Point. The lighthouse keeper there found him asleep on the sand the next morning, utterly exhausted.

Although that and his next venture, a commercial fishing operation at Marquette, also ended in failure, McDougall was by no means down and out. Ultimately, his name would be forever linked with the unique ships he invented and built, some of the most revolutionary vessels to ever ride the waves of the big lakes—the whalebacks.

Born March 16, 1845, on the island of Islay, off the west coast of Scotland, McDougall experienced a youth of poverty and little formal education. At the age of nine, he immigrated with his family to a small Scottish settlement on the shore of Georgian Bay near Collingwood, Ontario.

Shortly thereafter, his father was killed in a sawmill accident and the support of his mother and four siblings fell heavily on his slim shoulders. At the age of 14, he went to work full time on a farm, and he was later apprenticed to a blacksmith. In 1861, like many another Scottish lad, he took to the sea, securing a position as a deckhand on a steamer making the Collingwood to Chicago run.

He soon rose to the rank of first mate, sailing in that capacity aboard the Detroit-based Meteor from 1867 to 1870. By the following season, McDougall had proved his worthiness to command a wooden freighter, the Thomas A. Scott.

He became the master of successively larger ships until his temporary unemployment in 1875, which resulted in his ill-fated Upper Peninsula ventures. By late 1875, however, he was back at the helm, in command of the steamer City of Duluth. He celebrated the return of good luck by marrying a young Scottish lass from Toronto.

In 1880, McDougall supervised the construction, at Gilbraltar, Michigan, of the steamer Hiawatha and the barge Minnehaha, the largest wooden vessels to sail the Great Lakes. He commanded those vessels during the following two seasons, conveying railroad iron to Lake Superior.

During that period, he "thought out a plan to build an iron boat cheaper than wooden vessels...to carry the greatest cargo on the least water." Legend has it that the concept of the whaleback came to him during a dream, a dream in which he saw a low lying, cigar-shaped vessel plowing undaunted through great waves.

Be that as it may, by 1881 when McDougall had quit the life of a seaman to conduct a stevedore business in Duluth, he secured his first patent for a tow barge with a revolutionary hull design. It was flat-bottomed, semi-cylindrical and pointed on both ends.

But financial backing to build the first of what he dubbed the whaleback vessels proved elusive. Upon seeing one of McDougall's test models, one ship-owner reportedly snorted, "You call that damn thing a boat—why it looks more like a pig!" Pig-boats, in fact, became the popular, albeit pejorative term for McDougall's invention.

Despite such negative reactions, McDougall believed in his dream and he persevered. In 1888, he launched at Duluth a 191-foot whaleback barge, financed through his own capital. The maiden voyage of the vessel, loaded with iron ore, proved so successful that McDougall convinced Colgate Hoyt of the Rockefeller empire to back the formation of a company to construct additional whalebacks.

Four other barges were launched at Duluth before the first self-propelled whaleback, gratefully named the Colgate Hoyt, slid into Lake Superior in 1890. Ultimately, 40 whaleboats were constructed on the Great Lakes and four more at saltwater ports. Sixteen of the 44 were steamships and the remainder barges. In 1897, the last of the whalebacks was built, 412-foot-long and appropriately named the Alexander McDougall.

McDougall's dream had become reality. Whaleboats proved themselves seaworthy in the roughest weather, consumed about half the fuel of a standard-hulled vessel of the same carrying capacity and their many hatches made loading and unloading easier and faster. The whalebacks soon became popular with shippers.

Sailors, however, nursed a hatred of pig-boats, and captains were often hard pressed to fill out a crew. Part of the problem came from design defects: cramped quarters, bad ventilation and limited topside movement especially in bad weather. And, although there was no basis for the belief, sailors maintained that pig-boats would turn turtle easily—that they were man-killers.

What ultimately sealed the fate of the whaleback, however, was that they were simply too small to continue to compete with the leviathan freighters developed after the turn of the century. Another defect lay in the size of the hatches, too small to accommodate the huge clamshell unloaders that came into use. Nevertheless, four whaleback freighters continued in use through 1957.

But the grandest of the whalebacks, and the only one of its kind, was a passenger vessel. Launched in1892 at Superior, Wisconsin, the Christopher Columbus was built expressly to convey the millions of excursionists who thronged Chicago in 1893 to attend the Colombian Exposition Fairgrounds at Jackson Park. An opulently fitted-out vessel containing four decks replete with etched glass, velvet rugs, Corinthian leather upholstery and an Italian-marbled Grand Salon, the Columbus left Superior loaded with 7,500 passengers on its maiden voyage down the lakes to Chicago. As she neared the Straits, "a salute of twelve guns from Fort Mackinaw hailed the passing monster."

The Columbus transported 1.7 million exposition visitors during 1893 alone, and during her 40 years of sailing, she carried more passengers than any other vessel in the history of the Great Lakes. Sadly, the magnificent vessel was scrapped in 1936 and the steel sold to Japan.

In 1972, the last surviving whaleboat, the 366-foot Meteor, was towed back to the city of its birth to become a permanent maritime exhibit in Superior, Wisconsin.

No other American vessel, with the exception of the clipper ship, has inspired such a mystique as the whaleback. Wrote George C. Mason in 1953:

"The whaleback she was something
Beyond a seamen's ken
The like of her was never seen
Since ships were sailed by men."

Perry Whiting, Young River Hog

A logging scene near Boyne City in the 1880's.

Rousted out of his warm bunk early one spring morning in 1882, Perry Whiting pulled on his caulked boots, slipped into his Mackinaw jacket and made a bee-line for the cookhouse, where he and 15 other shanty-boys soon vanquished heaping platters of fried salt pork, flap-jacks smothered in black-strap molasses and big steaming mugs of strong coffee.

Then, he grabbed his peavey, a long-handled cant hook, and headed up the banks of Deer Creek, a stream which empties into the Jordan River, upstream from the sawmill town of East Jordan in southern Charlevoix County.

Whiting was a "river hog," as lumberjacks called those whose dangerous occupation was to ride logs downstream to the sawmills, retrieving beached logs and breaking up logjams along the way.

Jams, tangled piles of logs sometimes stretching a quarter of a mile upstream, acted like huge dams. The pent-up force of the logs and water behind was terrific. A skilled riverman could clamber across the jam, locate the "key log," pry and roll it free with his peavey, and when the jam broke loose, leap across the rolling, pitching logs to the safety of the shore. Those who fell were frequently ground to death or drowned beneath the tumbling avalanche of logs.

Despite the danger, 14-year-old Whiting, like most healthy boys, took his fun where he could find it.

He had been paired off with his uncle, Ben Healey, a jolly but quick-tempered man who could not get along with the other French-Canadian lumberjacks. Healey hated falling in the stream. That worry made him all the more awkward, and he usually managed to topple into the drink at least once a day. Consequently, he preferred to send his nephew out to break up logjams, and that is where Whiting had his fun.

Making his way out onto the jam, Whiting would locate the key log, twist and budge it until it was just ready to break free, fasten the jaws of his peavey into the log, put

162

his shoulder under the handle and pretend to be lifting as hard as he could. Then, he would call for his uncle to help him.

Picking his way gingerly across the jam, Healey would fix his peavey into the log and start to lift. At that moment, Whiting would give the log a quick roll and cause the jam to start to break. Terror-stricken, Healey would race for one bank, usually taking a ducking in the icy water before reaching shore. Taking the precaution to choose the opposite bank, Whiting would enjoy a hearty laugh, punctuated by his uncle's threats and curses.

Whiting described his logging experiences in an autobiography published in 1930. He fondly remembered life on the river: "There was something doing every moment, a jam to break, an argument, a fight, a song, someone in the river, something that made the day seem short and interesting."

Though but a boy at the time, Whiting was no stranger to the world of work. Born in 1868 in a log cabin in Lapeer County, he was the son of a northern Michigan lumberjack. When he was two years old, the family pioneered a densely forested tract on the shores of Pine Lake (now Lake Charlevoix), one mile north of Advance. The task of scraping a living out of the harsh northern wilderness required all family members, even small children, to pull their weight. By the time he was four, Whiting worked beside his father in the fields planting potatoes.

His father died that year from the effects of exposure incurred while wading for hours in an icy creek spearing suckers for use as fertilizer. Forced to go to work in a local shingle mill to support herself and unable to take care of the boy, his mother gave him up to family members.

Whiting got his first taste of "book learning" at the age of six in a tiny log schoolhouse, but education was not allowed to interfere with his work duties. He earned his first money when he was eight by picking a two-quart pint of wild raspberries, which he sold at a general store for 10 cents.

163

Soon, he was picking bushels of tomatoes and rowing them across the lake to Boyne City, where he exchanged them for groceries. He also carried on a lively trade with the various lumber schooners which plied the lake, rowing out to swap fresh milk for corn beef or whatever they had on board.

The winter he was eight, Whiting first went to work in the timber. His job was to chain a horse to small cedar trees the lumberjacks had chopped down and drag them out of the woods to be loaded on bobsleds and eventually cut into fence posts. He soon became adept at working horses and oxen and earned his own livelihood hauling freight and passengers, plowing gardens and other odd jobs.

Five years later, he rejoined his mother and step-father in Muskegon. There, he got a job with the Muskegon Boom Co. at $1.25 per 12-hour workday. At the booming grounds, located along the shores of Muskegon Lake, sorters using long-handled pike poles identified the owner-ship of various logs through distinctive log marks hammered onto their ends, separated them into floating enclosures known as booms and chained them together into rafts that were towed to the numerous sawmills that lined the banks of the lake.

Unfortunately, late that fall, Whiting slipped into the icy water while running across some logs, took a chill while walking the three miles home in wet clothes and developed pneumonia. He recovered three weeks later, but by that time, the river had frozen over, ending the booming season.

He returned to Charlevoix County, where he spent a long winter working in the woods, felling trees with a double-bitted axe, bucking them into 16-foot lengths with a two-man crosscut saw, skidding them out of the woods, piling great bobsled loads with a cant hook and transporting them to the banking grounds adjacent the river to await the river drive the next spring—where his fun with his uncle began.

Whiting again joined his mother, who had moved to Grand Rapids, when he was 16. He began attending school

164

there in earnest. In addition to that, he delivered newspapers, lit city street lights and worked as a janitor at the South Congregational Church. After graduation from high school at the age of 20, Whiting left Michigan for California.

In Los Angeles, he launched a building-material empire that eventually made him a very rich man. Despite his success, a half-century later, he remembered his glorious experiences as a Michigan river hog as the best days of his life.

Lyman E. Stowe, Detroit Visionary

In 1884, Lyman E. Stowe's conception of war in the 20th century featured jet-like fighter planes.

A gigantic bowl of steel and glass stretches 25 miles along the Detroit River and 10 miles inland on either side. Beneath that dome lies the city of Detroit/Windsor—Canada having long since accepted the inevitable and joined the American Union.

There, the happy denizens of Detroit enjoy a perfectly regulated environment, "lit up with various colored lights, preferable to sun-light, heated by electricity and the internal heats of the earth, brought up through tubes." Tropical fruit trees and flowers line the city's park-like avenues. Sedate strollers breathe "lovely breezes of pure air, loaded with a lovely aroma, sweet, pure and healthy."

If this does not sound like the Detroit you know, take heart—the city still has more than a century left to clean up its act. That is, if you accept the predictions penned in 1884 by poet, philosopher and Gratiot Avenue picture dealer, Lyman E. Stowe. Stowe published his view of Detroit in the year 2100 in a beautifully bound but little-read masterpiece, *Poetical Drifts of Thought or Problems of Progress,* a compendium of his futuristic prose and poetry, "embellished with nearly 200 illustrations."

Stowe's father, also name Lyman, had emigrated from Vermont to Michigan territory in the early 1830's. His mother hailed from western New York state. They were among the earliest pioneers to settle in Flint, where Stowe was born on April 2, 1843.

The weather on the day of his birth seemed to Stowe's parents to portend greatness for their offspring. By evening, an unseasonably warm wind had entirely melted the three feet of snow that blanketed the ground.

Unfortunately, the ensuing wet spring spawned more than the usual numbers of mosquitoes, which infected the infant with malaria. Racked by fever and chills for two years, Stowe later concluded that the disease may have rendered him "not as brilliant as I otherwise would have been."

Be that as it may, Stowe may also have inherited a

degree of eccentricity from his father, who served as Flint's first postmaster, carrying the mail around under his high top hat and handing out letters as he chanced upon their recipients. Sadly, the elder Stowe died in 1852, leaving his widow with a large family of small children. The poverty they endured prevented Stowe from attending even grade school.

When the Civil War broke out in April 1861, Stowe rushed to join the colors, enlisting in Company F, 2nd Michigan Infantry Regiment, formed of Flint men. At that time, he could barely write his own name. Nevertheless, during the three years he served with the regiment, participating in many of the stirring battles of the war, he taught himself to read by perusing dime novels and newspapers.

When the war ended, Stowe settled in Detroit, where he earned his livelihood selling books door-to-door and operating a retail print shop. During the succeeding two decades, he honed his education by reading everything he could lay his hands on. By 1884, he was ready to share with his countrymen the imaginative theories he had conceived.

Acknowledging, however, that "I have read so much that I can hardly say where all my ideas came from or what is my own or what I have borrowed from others," he took the precaution of inserting a bold-faced set of quotation marks in the volume's preface so that fastidious readers could place them where they belonged.

Filled with atrocious poetry, bad grammar and simplistic explanations, Stowe's volume describing life in the future might be completely laughed off were it not for the nagging fact that many of his predictions have indeed come to pass. Nineteen years before the Wright brothers made the first successful airplane flight, Stowe envisioned a jet-type aircraft. Wars of the future, including the battle that would end war forever, would, he predicted, feature those aircraft dropping bombs on cities. Other weapons of the future included cannons able to hurl laser-type beams of destruction.

A full decade before the discovery of the X-ray, Stowe wrote of "a means of lighting up the human body with electricity in such a manner that the physician or surgeon can clearly see the field in which he is to operate." Four decades before television became a reality, Stowe described "a large disc of white burnished metal" upon which electricity conveyed vibrations of light "so that it is practicable not only to speak with a distant friend, but to see him.

For his hometown of Detroit, already suffering in 1884 from pollution, widespread crime and urban ugliness, Stowe conjectured a 21st century Utopia. Factories, "where everybody will work a few hours each day," would be banished outside the confines of the Eden-like dome city. There would be "no poverty, no extreme wealth, no poorhouses, no prisons, no graveyards." Dead bodies would be cremated and their chemical elements re-utilized.

The causes of poverty and crime would be eliminated, thus removing the need for such non-productive occupations as soldiers, judges, lawyers and police. Those few sociopaths who persisted in crime would be put to a speedy, painless death, hence a solution to overcrowded prisons.

Stowe's volume appears not to have made much of a splash in 1884. Eventually, his wife Mildred took over its distribution. What few copies were printed have since been relegated to rare-book collections.

What happened to Stowe, the social dreamer, is open to conjecture. He mentions in a footnote that having discovered a new principle of flight, he "had in contemplation a flying machine that he believes would work perfectly, and which he will soon test."

Was Stowe's fate to plummet to his death or to soar to new flights of prophetic fancy?

Talking Turkey

*"The last wild turkey in Michigan", a gobbler weighing 23 3/4 pounds,
was shot by William Mershon near Saginaw in 1886.*

William B. Mershon did not think much of those who called turkeys and then shot them from cover—that lacked sportsmanship. He preferred to track the big birds down and shoot them on the wing—and he had gotten plenty that way. Yet, of all the remarkable experiences the sportsman had garnered during his 50 years of hunting and fishing, none was more memorable than the time he "killed the last wild turkey in Michigan."

It was mid-November 1886, and Mershon, proprietor of a Saginaw planing mill and saltworks, had taken the day off to go partridge shooting with a friend.

The two had boarded a Detroit and Bay City Railroad train that morning and gotten off at a little station nine or 10 miles east of Saginaw, intending to hunt from there to Reese in Tuscola County, where they could catch an afternoon train back home. Although they did not expect to encounter anything other than ruffed grouse, they had taken the precaution to pack along a few shells loaded with No. 2 shot just in case they found a wild turkey. The sportsmen knew the big birds had been hunted to near extinction, but in years past that region had "been the very heart and cream of the wild turkey district."

About a half mile from the railroad, Mershon's old Gordon setter, Bob, flushed a couple of partridges, which the hunters had shot. Then, in the light dusting of snow that had fallen the night before, they spied the fresh tracks of three turkeys—big tracks, too. The men quickly slipped the heavier turkey loads into their double-barreled shotguns and began following the trail. But two hours later, the sun had melted off the snow, and they lost the tracks.

The hunters returned to banging away at partridges, and by mid-afternoon, their pockets each bulged with four to five birds. Before they called it a day, they decided to make one more sweep through the section where they had seen the turkey tracks.

Suddenly, Bob came to a point at a big elm tree. An instant later, a huge gobbler flapped out of the treetop.

171

Mershon nailed him with one round at 30 yards. Bob valiantly tried to fetch the big bird, which "thrashed around like a chicken with its head cut off," but it was too much for him.

When the turkey had ended its death throes, Mershon tied a string to its head and feet and proudly packed it the three miles to Reese. His trophy weighed in at 23 3/4 pounds. Mounted, it became the prize of his stuffed bird collection, "radiant as an Oriental jewel box."

Indigenous only to North America, the eastern wild turkey is the continent's largest upland game bird, sometimes reaching over 30 pounds. Its original range extended from northern Florida to Maine and the lower Great Lakes region and west to the Great Plains.

Most Indians considered turkey a delicacy, although some tribes thought the hunting of the big birds a sport to be practiced only by children. The only Indians who domesticated turkeys were the Aztec of Mexico. Following his sacking of that empire, Hernando Cortes first introduced the turkey to Europe during the early 16th century.

The British colonists who settled the Atlantic seaboard found wild turkeys in abundance. Such game was a welcome addition to many a frontier larder. Beginning with the first Thanksgiving Day celebrated by the Pilgrims at Plymouth Colony in 1621, turkey came to be particularly associated with that feast. Turkeys remained plentiful throughout the 18th century. Ornithologist John James Audubon recorded that, in Kentucky in about 1800, a 10- to 12-pound bird sold for only six cents.

Despite that low price, by the early 19th century, professional market hunters had begun to make inroads on the turkey population. Turkeys had been wiped out in Connecticut by 1813, Vermont by 1842 and Massachusetts by 1851. By 1872, the market price in Chicago for wild turkeys had reached $1 while at the same time wild geese brought less than 40 cents.

Michigan pioneers found turkeys most plentiful south of

172

a line drawn from Saginaw to Muskegon. J.S. Tibbits, who settled in Wayne County's Livonia Township in the 1820's, recalled that "vast flocks of several hundred were frequently to be met with." He and a companion killed "seven large fine birds" in one day alone.

Pioneers employed various techniques to take turkeys. Some tracked them down one by one, as Mershon favored. Others, when encountering a flock, fired randomly into it to cause the turkeys to scatter in all directions. They knew the hens would invariably return to the site to locate their young who hid in the underbrush. Secreting themselves and mimicking the pipings of the mother bird with a call fashioned from the hollow bone of a turkey wing, the hunters lured the old birds into range. After they had been shot, it was an easy matter to pick off the young birds as well.

Some pioneers also trapped turkeys in covered pens made of poles. They scattered grain inside and around a passageway that was just high enough to admit one turkey. Pecking at the bait, the birds would enter the pen heads down. Once inside and standing erect, they could see no way out. Not a particularly bright bird, it seems, they would never lower their heads to find the passageway out.

Wild turkeys remained fairly common throughout much of southern Michigan as late as 1875. But during the next decade, destruction of the forests, coupled with intense hunting by farmers, sportsmen and professional market hunters, brought about their rapid demise.

Contrary to his statement, Mershon did not kill the last wild turkey in Michigan—but it was one of the last. A few wild turkeys were reported in Kalamazoo County in 1888 and Allegan County in 1892. One was seen near Hudsonville in Kent County in 1897, and that same year, a gobbler was shot in VanBuren County.

Conservation measures adopted by the state Legislature proved too little, too late. A law passed in1889 prohibited the killing of wild turkeys except in October and November. A revision of the game laws passed in 1901 placed a moratorium on the killing of turkeys until 1910. Unfortunately, by 1900, the birds already had been hunted to extinction in Michigan.

Despite his zeal in killing one of the last of the breed, Mershon lamented that the "grand, glorious game birds...are gone forever here in Michigan."

In 1954, the Michigan Department of Conservation released 50 turkeys acquired from Pennsylvania into the Allegan State Forest. For some unknown reason, those chosen to restock the Allegan State Forest were a game-farm variety rather than live-trapped wild birds. Studies of restocking efforts in Virginia during the 1930's had demonstrated that game-farm birds would not thrive in the wild.

Additional restocking attempts in later years using wild-trapped turkeys, particularly in the northern Lower Peninsula, have brought better results. Currently, an estimated 40,000 wild turkeys range over some 10,000 square miles of Michigan.

Those fortunate enough to catch a glimpse of a wild turkey in a natural setting will readily understand why Benjamin Franklin advocated the majestic bird as America's national symbol.

George Shiras, Pioneer Nature Photographer

George Shiras' pioneering night photograph of a rare albino porcupine in the Marquette vicinity.

The north woods rustled with the nocturnal prowlings of the creatures of the wild. Deer, beaver, raccoon and porcupine foraged in peace, unaware that their sanctuary had been violated, that a hunter had laid a snare to capture their souls.

Suddenly, the night exploded in a blaze of light. A doe and twin fawns browsing at the lakeshore had triggered the trap. In terror, they bounded for safety. But it was too late, they had been taken, frozen forever on a photographic plate.

Thus did George Shiras III, pioneer nature photographer, stalk his quarry. In an era when Michigan's game animals were rapidly being driven to near extinction, he first demonstrated that photographic hunters might enjoy all the thrills of the chase save the sanguineous end results. What's more, the trophies Shiras mounted and displayed won him worldwide acclaim as a photographer and naturalist.

Born in Pittsburgh in 1859, Shiras came from a long line of sportsmen. His grandfather, the first George Shiras, had been lured to the north country in quest of its fabled trout fishing. Beginning in 1849, he established a vacation headquarters at Marquette, and he returned for the succeeding 45 seasons. A decade later, his son, George Shiras II, also began making yearly pilgrimages to the region. Shiras III, who had grown up tramping the Pennsylvania woods with rod and gun, first came to Marquette at the age of 11, in 1870. He, too, fell in love with the unspoiled beauty of the Upper Peninsula.

Shiras graduated from Cornell University in 1881, and two years later, completed a law degree at Yale. Entering his father's law firm, he eventually took it over. He served as a member of the Pennsylvania Legislature in 1889-90 and in the U.S. Congress in 1903-05. Despite his successful professional life, his heart remained in the north country. Each summer, he found relief from the industry-polluted Ohio Valley in the crystal clear air and water of the Upper Peninsula.

During his second summer in the Upper Peninsula, an

Indian guide name Joe La Pete led the 12-year-old Shiras to a beautiful little lake he had discovered about 20 miles east of Marquette. Shiras named it Whitefish Lake, and on its shore, he established his hunting camp and later the family cottage. Deer and other game animals abounded in the vicinity of Whitefish Lake, and Shiras enjoyed many youthful hunting adventures.

By the late 1880's, however, the urge to kill had become "subordinated to the sympathetic desire of the naturalist to know more of the lives, habits and mentality of the wild things he so often encountered." In 1889, Shiras laid aside his gun. Instead, "the father of wildlife photography" originated and promoted the sport of hunting with the camera.

He first attempted to photograph deer from a canoe in daytime. Next, he mounted a camera at a likely spot and at the approach of a subject, pulled a long string from concealment, which tripped the shutter. Finally, he devised a trip-wire method which freed him from many tedious hours of waiting.

Although he managed some excellent photographs during the daytime, his greatest successes came at night. A favorite method of hunting deer during that era, and one that was perfectly legal, was to jacklight deer from a canoe. Deer have the unfortunate tendency to stare stupidly at an approaching bright light, thus making them easy prey for night hunters. Shiras adapted this technique by which market hunters were decimating the deer population to photograph wild creatures.

The photographic technology of the time required the use of magnesium powder, which, when ignited, flamed with a brilliant light. Despite the clumsy nature of this method, Shiras succeeded in taking the first successful "flash light" photograph of a wild animal, a yearling buck standing on the lakeshore, in 1891. Later, he invented a pistol-like apparatus for firing the powder, which permitted more reliable results.

Next, Shiras adapted his trip-wire method to night photography. Animals prowling in the dark tripped a wire that simultaneously set off the powder charge and snapped the camera shutter. Some of his most spectacular night photographs were of the albino deer herd that lived on Grand Island, off Munising.

In 1901, Shiras recorded one of his most amazing sets of photographs—an albino porcupine. The photographs attracted much attention because only one other such specimen had been previously discovered. Several naturalists urged Shiras to kill the rare animal for display in a museum. Instead, Shiras returned during the succeeding five summers to record the animal in its natural habitat.

During that process, he discovered that the animal was blind and deaf. It is doubtful that any animal other than a porcupine, whose sharp quills protect it from predators, could have survived in the wild with those handicaps. The creature holed up in a hollow log during the daytime and at night ventured out to locate the plants and bark it fed on by sense of touch and smell. In 1904, Shiras photographed the albino mother and her offspring, a normal, dark-colored baby, on a log together.

Shiras' wildlife photographs received the highest awards at the Paris World Exposition in 1900 and the Louisiana Purchase Exposition at St. Louis in 1904. Beginning in 1906, with an illustrated essay entitled "Photographing Wild Animals with Flashlight and Camera," Shiras contributed a long series of popular articles to *National Geographic Magazine*. Many leading sportsmen, including President Theodore Roosevelt, began supporting Shiras' philosophy that "game to the rifle is game to the camera."

Roosevelt wrote him in 1906 that "no other work you can do is as important as for you to write a big book" based on his photographs and natural history notes.

In 1935, the National Geographic Society published Shiras' collected works and 950 of his photographs in two large volumes, a monument to the life-work of America's pioneer nature photographer.

Harry Smith's
Fifty Years of Slavery

Harry Smith, who had lived as a slave for 50 years, in 1891.

He was "a long, lean, lantern-jawed, lobered-mouthed, high-cheeked Englishman, knock-kneed and club-footed, with no hair on his head, and lived about four miles west of Reed City."

Those faults notwithstanding, he might have continued to enjoy his peaceful mug of beer in a fashionable Reed City saloon had he not also been a loud-mouthed bigot. "You, you nigger, come here, come here nigger, come here," he bawled across the bar, addressing Harry Smith.

Smith, who had spent 50 years in slavery in Kentucky among overseers who made Simon Legree look like Santa Claus, was not about to take that insult—not in Michigan anyway. Raising a heavy bar stool over his head, Smith told him that if he opened his mouth in such a way again, he "would smash him into the floor and never stop to sharpen him." The bigot became a believer and never bothered Smith again.

Smith described that incident, as well as how he made short work of several other Reed City racists, in an autobiographical volume published in Grand Rapids in 1891. But the major portion of his 183-page *Fifty Years of Slavery in the United States of America* records the horrors of that "peculiar institution" as witnessed by Smith.

Born into slavery in 1815 in a weaving loom shed on a plantation in Nelson County, Kentucky, Smith was one of 18 siblings. His mother, a pious Catholic, saw to it that all her children were christened in the local Catholic church. Her religion, however, did not protect her from being treated in a most barbaric manner by the white man who owned her.

One of Smith's earliest memories was of crying and begging the master not to kill his mother as, tied to a tree in front of the house with her clothing stripped from her body, she received 100 whip lashes, each one drawing blood. Her offense had been to take a 10-minute rest break while cutting corn.

Her punishment was light compared to that meted out to

180

an old slave on the neighboring Ray plantation who had run away and been captured. Uncle George, as he was called, "was stripped naked, bound in the henhouse directly under their droppings, taken out, received 100 lashes from Ray, the same from his son, and placed back under the roost naked, face up. The next morning, (he) received the same with his flesh all lacerated, was bound to a shovel plow to cultivate tobacco, compelled to do a hard day's work."

Another nearby slave master named Edward Brisco won a well-deserved reputation for his cruelty. His philosophy was: "It didn't matter how good they were, they must be whipped once a year to let them know they were negroes." To prove his point, a few days before one Christmas, he had two of his loyal slaves, each more than 70 years old, stripped, bent over a barrel and given 50 lashes for no offense whatsoever. Other plantation owners frequently sent him slaves who gave them behavior problems for punishment.

Perhaps the most fiendish of the many Kentucky slave owners described by Smith was David L. Ward, the "hell hawk." He owned 300 slaves who worked his extensive salt manufacturing plant. Once, when he discovered a few pounds of salt had been left to burn on the bottom of a kettle, he bashed the slave responsible on the head with a shovel, then pitched him into the furnace to burn to death. His old slaves witnessed him "at different times, burn up in his furnace 15 colored people."

The actual murder of slaves, those able to work, anyway, was evidently a rare occurrence. With an individual slave worth $2,000 or more on the market, they were too valuable a commodity to be destroyed. Oftentimes, slaves were rented out to those who needed extra labor. If someone killed a slave belonging to another, he could be sued for damages—the value of the slave reckoned at the going rate per year times his expected life span. The murder of a young slave might cost the killer several thousand dollars.

Normally, according to Smith, if whipping or other cruel punishment did not bring unruly or insubordinate slaves under control, they were sold down the river to New Orleans, a fate greatly feared by Kentucky slaves.

Smith's own 50 years spent as a slave were happier than most. Following his cruel master's death, he was acquired by Master and Mrs. Jack Salone, who treated him kindly. That Smith was a hard worker who seldom incurred their displeasure also helped.

Several times during forays to visit girlfriends on neighboring plantations, however, he ran afoul of vigilantes known as "patrollers." They would capture and whip any slave out and about without a written pass from his owner. Smith, who was known as the fastest runner in the county, successfully eluded patrollers on several occasions, although once, a vicious bloodhound nailed him. He carried the scars from that close call to his dying day.

In 1861, Smith's white countrymen went to war to determine whether slavery would continue. He witnessed many atrocities committed by the guerrilla bands that roamed Kentucky during the succeeding four years. He assisted in burying 50 slaves, for example, who were gunned down while en route to the Union lines. Smith risked his own life to assist Union stragglers and parolees in hiding out from the bloodthirsty guerrillas.

Then, one morning in 1863 following President Abraham Lincoln's Emancipation Proclamation, Smith's master walked in while the slaves were eating breakfast, steadied himself against a table and sadly announced:

"Men and women hear me, I am about to tell you something I never expected to be obliged to tell you in my life, it is this: it becomes my duty to inform you, one and all, women, men and children, belonging to me, you are free to go where you please." Never had a scene been witnessed on the plantation to rival the resulting freedom jubilee.

After the war, Smith and his family moved to a farm 12 miles north of Indianapolis, where he sharecropped for a white landowner. In 1872, while on a hunting expedition, he first visited Reed City, a frontier settlement then known as Todd's Slashing. Although few of the settlers there had ever seen a black man before, Smith soon won acceptance through his great sense of humor and warm personality.

He bought a lot and the following March moved to Reed City with his family. Times were tough, but he earned a living cutting cord wood while his wife and daughter set up a laundry business. Two years later, they had saved $50, enough to make a down payment on 20 acres of wilderness land located three and one half miles north of town in Lincoln Township.

Smith built a house and gradually cleared his homestead while his family continued to do laundry, which Smith carried in large baskets on his head back and forth to Reed City. Eventually, he succeeded in paying off his farm and in erecting a dance hall, 100 feet long.

For many years, settlers for miles around flocked to Smith's dance hall to "trip the light fantastic toe" to the tune of his tambourine and to listen to his amazing stories of 50 years of life in slavery.

The Sinking of the Chicora

The ill-fated Chicora, pride of the Graham and Morton Line.

The telegraph clerk listened intently to the clacking of the key, deftly translating the dots and dashes into words. It was an urgent message from the boss, John Graham, co-owner of the St. Joseph-based Graham & Morton Steamship Line. The clerk raced down the dock along the Milwaukee River where the Chicora had just cast off its moor lines and was slowly steaming off.

He yelled at the top of his voice: "Mr. Graham says to stay in port—there's a big storm coming." But no one on board heard him, and the lights of the vessel grew dimmer and dimmer as it turned out into Milwaukee Harbor.

It was the morning of January 21, 1895, an unseasonably warm day with scarcely a breeze. But Graham had reacted to what should have alerted the Chicora's captain, Edward Stines, as well—the barometer was falling very fast, in fact, it touched 28, a sure sign of an impending storm and a bad one.

Perhaps Stines had felt the Chicora, a new and exceptionally strong vessel, could take the worst the Big Lake might dish out. With luck, the ship would make it to St. Joseph in six hours.

Launched in the Detroit River in the spring of 1892, the Chicora, nearly 200 feet in length and 35 feet in breadth, had been specially constructed to withstand the rigors of winter travel on the Great Lakes. Her wooden outer hull consisted of six inch planking, reinforced with a steel bumper guard at the water line designed to fend off ice. Below deck, she was divided into three self-contained compartments, each able to be sealed off in the event of a leak. Her huge steam engine, rated as one of the most powerful on the lakes, could push her along at 20 miles per hour. So confident were her owners that she was unsinkable that they carried no marine insurance.

Capable of conveying 1,200 passengers as well as heavy cargo, the "pride of the fleet" plied the St. Joseph to Chicago route during the tourist season and transported freight to Milwaukee in the winter.

185

Her second season, 1893, proved a boom year, as thousands of excursionists thronged the Chicora's opulently furnished cabins and 100-foot main lounge for a visit to the Colombian Exposition in Chicago. The following year brought another profitable accident-free season.

Because of lack of freight in early January 1895, the Chicora lay idle in St. Joseph harbor for the first time in her nearly three years. Then, on January 19, Graham received a frantic telegraph from Milwaukee. A backlog of freight had built up a the wharf there. He promised to send the Chicora over as soon as possible.

Chief engineer, Robert McClure, fired up the boiler while Graham alerted the other 24 crew members that they would sail at noon the next day. One was ill, however, and another was on his honeymoon. But Graham rounded up substitutes, one of whom asked permission to bring along a friend, Joseph F. Pearl, a young St. Joseph druggist.

The Chicora steamed out of St. Joseph Harbor right on schedule on January 20. Only one incident marred the routine six-hour voyage to Milwaukee. Pearl, an avid sportsman, had brought his rifle along. When he spied a mallard flying straight toward the vessel, he fired and brought it down.

The sailors stood aghast. Since ducks rarely approached a steamer, Pearl's action seemed akin to killing an albatross, a la the ancient mariner. Capt. Stines reportedly slammed Pearl against a lifeboat and shouted, "My God, Pearl, what have you done? I feel like kneeling down and offering up a prayer."

Pearl's blunder cast a pall over the crew, a somber mood that continued even as the Chicora made the harbor and steamed up the Milwaukee River to the wharf. It would take at least 10 hours for dockworkers to fill the Chicora's holds with bags of flour, 632 tons in all. Yet, so distraught were the superstitious sailors that most chose to remain on board rather than enjoy a spree in "the city that made beer famous."

186

At 5:45 a.m. the next day, the Chicora cast off. Nearly three hours later, the U.S. Weather Service in Chicago issued a storm warning. A hurricane strength blizzard which had demolished several southern towns was tracking directly toward Lake Michigan.

The temperature dropped 35 degrees that morning in Chicago, and by noon, 60 mph winds battered the Windy City. In Muskegon, rain turned to sleet then snow, a total of four feet. Benton Harbor's oldest residents had never seen the like of such a fierce gale.

Noon on the 21st came and went with no sign of the Chicora. As day turned into night, anxious friends and relatives climbed the highest hilltops to scan the Big Lake for signs of the vessel. Hope remained strong that she would turn up safe and secure at some other port of refuge or that she was merely locked in the ice that stretched far out, an eventuality that her strong hull had been built to withstand.

After the storm subsided, some of her sister ships scoured the lake in search of the Chicora. Then, late in the afternoon of January 22, a search party walking the beach north of South Haven stumbled onto a large piece of wreckage, positively identified as from the Chicora's pilothouse.

Nevertheless, Graham and others remained optimistic that the Chicora's hull was intact and crew still safe —somewhere. But as the month wore on, other small bits of wreckage from the vessel turned up.

The nation's attention seemed focused on the fate of the Chicora. Newspapers hurried into special edition with stories of cottagers sighting the vessel or hearing its steam whistle. A little Skye terrier, identified as the ship's mascot, appeared out of nowhere to scratch on the door of a cottage eight miles north of St. Joseph.

Then, on February 1 came joyous tidings. The Chicora's hull had been sighted frozen in the ice off the coast of Whiting, Indiana. Nineteen men were counted walking its deck. Amid massive preparations for the "rescue of the century," thousands of spectators rushed to Whiting. Graham dispatched a special investigator who arrived there at dusk. Early the next morning, the investigator trained powerful binoculars on the wreck and saw 19 seagulls standing on a large ice flow resembling a ship.

Periodically, other hoaxes or mistaken sightings made the news. But the exact fate of the "unsinkable" Chicora has never been revealed. Lake Michigan swallowed up her and her entire crew and spit out only bits of flotsam and no bodies. Based on where wreckage was found, most authorities theorize she went down somewhere near South Haven.

Graham, the crew's families and the community of St. Joseph ultimately accepted the inevitable. Popular songwriters wrote heart rending ballads about the tragedy. Nixon Waterman penned "Song and Sigh:" "Here's a sigh for the Chicora, for the broken, sad Chicora; Here's a tear for those who followed her beneath the tossing wave..."

A tiny southwestern Allegan County community ensured that the disaster would not be forgotten by naming itself Chicora.

In 1907, other pieces of wreckage from the Chicora were found. Ten years later, a tug steamed into St. Joseph harbor with a wash basin and electric light fixture stamped "Chicora," which it had dredged up. Although divers have searched for her wreck for decades, the Chicora remains one of Lake Michigan's most baffling mysteries.

Anna Howard Shaw, Champion of Women's Rights

Dr. Anna Howard Shaw, ca. 1893.

Hundreds of women and few male interlopers packed the opera house. A hush fell over the audience as the distinguished speaker advanced with a smile. A short stout woman of matronly bearing with white hair drawn back in a bun, her crossed ivory hands accented her glistening black gown. Dr. Anna Howard Shaw's dark eyes sparkled as she began to speak in a rich contralto voice:

"It has been argued that women were inferior to men because their brains weigh less. The quantity, not the quality, of brains is taken into consideration in this estimate. A man in the slums of Boston who killed himself by drinking 17 glasses of beer on a wager was found to have a larger brain than Daniel Webster."

The entire audience roared its approval of her wit. For the next hour, she held them spellbound, as one-by-one she demolished the ludicrous reasons advanced by men to deprive women of the right to vote. Shaw concluded her talk with a question-and-answer session. Drawing a question from a box that had been circulated among the audience, she read, "Why does the Scripture say that there shall be no marriages in Heaven?"

"Ah, my dear friends," she responded, sadly shaking her head and drawing a long sigh," someone has answered that by saying, because there will be no men there."

During her long career as a women's rights activist, which began in Michigan, Shaw delivered more than 10,000 temperance and suffrage speeches. Her keen sense of humor and ready wit often proved more effective than logic. Her platform performances, writings, pioneer efforts as a female minister and administrative talents earned her a ranking alongside Susan B. Anthony, Elizabeth Cady Stanton and Carrie Chapman Catt as one of the foremost leaders in the women's suffrage movement.

Of Scottish ancestry, she was born in Newcastle-on-Tyne, England, February 14, 1847. Four years later, her family immigrated to America, ultimately settling in Lawrence, Massachusetts. Her father, James, worked as a paper hanger until, in 1859, he caught the wanderlust again. With his eldest son, also named James, he traveled to the Michigan frontier, where he pre-empted 160 acres of timbered land in Green Township, Mecosta County.

After clearing a space in the forest and raising a log cabin, Shaw left his son to hold down the homestead while he returned to Lawrence. Two months later, he sent his wife and four children, including 12-year-old Anna, to their new home in the wilderness. He and two other sons would continue to work in Lawrence for another 18 months.

Mrs. Shaw and the four children traveled by rail to the end of the line, Grand Rapids, where they heaped a lumber wagon high with all their earthly possessions and lurched north over some of the most miserable roads in the state. It took seven days to make the approximately 60-mile journey to the homestead, located near present-day Paris. There, an unfinished log cabin without door, windows or floor awaited them. A path to their nearest neighbors wound six miles through untamed wilderness frequented by bears, wolves and an occasional panther. The harsh reality of their plight nearly drove Anna's mother insane.

To make matters worse, 20-year-old James Jr. soon grew ill and had to return to the East for an operation. That left Mrs. Shaw, her three daughters and an eight-year-old son alone to fend for themselves. Somehow, the family managed to survive by growing a small garden among the giant stumps, picking berries, and snaring fish, and through an occasional remittance sent by the father. During the first winter, when snow frequently drifted through the poorly chinked walls, the Shaws lived largely on corn meal, purchased and lugged from the closest gristmill—20 miles away.

Life got a little better when the family was reunited in 1861, but that lasted only briefly. The elder Shaw and two sons enlisted in the Union Army shortly after the Civil War broke out, leaving the women to shift for themselves again.

191

Although she had received but a few months of formal education in a nearby country schoolhouse, Anna secured a teaching job when she was 15. At a time when women were preferred as schoolteachers because they could be paid less than men, and school boards earned their laurels for how cheaply they paid teachers, Anna started at $2 a week plus board.

When her father returned from the war in 1865, Anna left the farm to live with a married sister in Big Rapids. There, she hoped to learn a trade and then save enough money to accomplish her long-cherished dream of getting a decent education. Soon, she entered the Big Rapids High School, where the curriculum included a course in elocution.

Shaw's first attempt at public speaking revealed little of her later platform brilliance. Stage struck, she stuttered out a few lines of poem, then fainted to the floor. But she returned to the podium 10 minutes later and bravely finished her piece.

Shaw joined the Methodist Church in Big Rapids in 1870, and at the request of a local minister who sensed her talent, she preached her first sermon in Ashton, Osceola County. That daring deed, considered sacrilegious by most Americans at that time, caused her family to disown her for several years. Nevertheless, Shaw was convinced she had found her life's work.

She began attending Albion College in 1872, working her way through by preaching. Three years later, she became the second woman ever to enter the theological school at Boston University. Following graduation in 1878, she served as pastor of the Methodist Episcopal Church at Higham, Massachusetts. The church hierarchy, however, refused to ordain her. She switched to the Protestant Methodist Church in 1880, becoming the first woman to be ordained by that denomination.

She took time out from her ministerial duties to earn a medical degree from Boston University in 1886. Shaw resigned her pastorate that year, not to practice medicine but to devote her full energies to women's suffrage.

During the succeeding three decades, she lectured across the nation on the Chautauqua circuit, earning a reputation as "the most moving and eloquent orator in the suffrage cause." Elected vice president of the National American Women's Suffrage Association in 1892, she succeeded Carrie Chapman Catt as its president 12 years later, holding that position until 1915. She received the Distinguished Service Medal in 1919 for her work during World War I.

Sadly, Shaw died on July 2, 1919, a year before the 19th Amendment, which finally granted women the right to vote, was ratified. Currently, efforts are under way to honor her achievements with a commemorative postage stamp.

The Saints of Grand Junction

Brother Enoch Byrum and daughter Birdie donned appropriate apparel during a trip to the Holy land in 1904.

Never had the "Saints of the Most High God" experienced the presence of such a multitude. Over 10,000 visitors had swelled the population of the tiny Van-Buren County community of Grand Junction in June 1895. They came to take part in the saints' revival camp meeting, a cross between church and carnival which had been Grand Junction's and nearby Bangor's big summer event for more than a decade.

Members of the Church of God, a Protestant sect founded with the objective of ending sectarianism and restoring church dogma to that which had been practiced by the primitive Christians, the saints coupled evangelical zeal with the power of the press. From their denominational press, The Gospel Trumpet Publishing Co. in Grand Junction flowed a torrent of tracts in English and German, a bimonthly periodical called *The Gospel Trumpet* as well as a series of hardbound volumes of poetry, hymns and sex guidance.

The saints' most distinctive trait, however, was their belief in faith healing. Their chief champion of that doctrine, a young Hoosier named Enoch E. Byrum, had arrived in Grand Junction in 1887 to succeed D.S. Warner as editor of *The Gospel Trumpet*. Byrum expounded his views on faith healing through the columns of that journal as well as in his 248-page book, *Divine Healing of Soul and Body*, published in Grand Junction in 1892.

Simply put, Byrum and the saints believed that the miracles of healing as performed by Christ and other biblical figures were still available to those of sufficient faith. Sickness was merely the work of the devil and not, as some other denominations maintained, a heaven-sent test of character. Those of faith could heal themselves through prayer or be made well by certain church elders blessed with the gift of healing hands. To consult regular physicians or to use medicine of any kind even in the most severe sickness implied a lack of faith that would spoil the cure.

The elders accomplished their miracles by anointing the head of the afflicted with olive oil following by the laying on of hands. Tough cases required as many as six or more elders to simultaneously take hold of the patient.

Byrum's book offers scores of testimonials from long suffering victims who had been made "whole again" through faith healing. Dreaded 19th century ailments such as La Grippe, catarrh and bloody flux as well as blindness, deafness and broken bones were frequently cured instantaneously. But it sometimes took several weeks following the laying on of hands for other diseases like cancer and consumption to release their hold on the patient. Sufferers residing at too great a distance from VanBuren County or too sick to travel might avail themselves of the saints' special offer delivered via the U.S. mail, "anointed handkerchiefs," which had by themselves frequently wrought curative wonders.

Brother Byrum himself was among those blessed with the power to heal, and he swore to have seen with his own eyes "thousands cured by such methods. What is more, he had exorcised genuine devils from patients. Those occult sessions had led him to conclude that "of the great number of people who are now in insane asylums, doubtless, most of them are possessed with devils."

Be that as it may, devils also, it seems, were at the root of the predicament which the saints found themselves in as the June 1895 camp meeting wore on. A goodly number, evidently, had been drawn there to cavort, ogle and otherwise do the devil's work rather than improve their spiritual well-being.

The night before the grand finale of the camp meeting, a Sunday of fasting and prayer, a young backslider in attendance had received a nasty kick by a horse, the hooves "striking him in the stomach and on the shoulder and breast, dislocating his left shoulder, cracking or breaking some of his ribs and knocking him senseless to the ground." He was carried unconscious to a coterie of elders

196

who soon manipulated him back to life. Once his name was ascertained, his mother was located on the grounds. She, it turned out, had been "saved" and was "a strong believer in divine healing."

Although the youth had once been saved, he had since reverted to his wicked ways. Nevertheless, he determined to place himself in the elders' hands, and they soon succeeded in setting his dislocated shoulder. In the meantime, however, some disbeliever had gone for a physician. The doctor arrived, conducted an examination and concluded "that there were serious internal injuries which were liable to cause death at almost any time." He bandaged the arm and shoulder of the youth who had, mercifully, lapsed back into unconsciousness.

That obviously would not do—for the elders to work their miracle, it would have to be "whole hog or nothing." When the youth again regained consciousness, he ripped the bandages off. Throughout that night and the following day, he suffered intense pain. The thousands who milled around the campground that afternoon observed his sufferings as the elders worked on him in an open tent.

Mobs of angry disbelievers formed to angrily argue the plight of the poor lad, bereft of medical attention. Some spoke loudly of tar and feathers for the elders. Others suggested perhaps a "necktie party" might be in order should the youth die.

Regardless of such threats, as Byrum described in an autobiographical account published 10 years later, the saints continued their ministrations, and by that afternoon, the youth had, they believed, acquired sufficient faith for the healing attempt. As a large crowd looked on, the elders anointed his head with olive oil and laid hands upon him. Immediately, he ceased gasping for breath. Stepping aside, the elders commanded him "to arise in the name of the Lord and be well."

He sat up, pulled on his shoes and vest and began walking about, as hale and hearty as ever a youth there was. To

197

demonstrate his complete recovery, he "smote his chest several blows upon the injured parts."

Although ugly rumors began circulating that the injured boy had actually died and been replace by a "ringer," the saints carried the day, and there was no necktie party in Grand Junction.

Partly in response to such successes, The Gospel Trumpet Publishing Co. grew by leaps and bounds. In 1897, more than 1,000 pounds of tracts were sent to India alone. By 1898, some 75 employees set type, ran the steam presses and bound books in a large factory adjacent the railroad tracks in Grand Junction.

Then suddenly, on June 28th of that year, the saints loaded all their belongings on a specially chartered train, climbed aboard and chugged out of Grand Junction, en route to a new headquarters in Moundsville, West Virginia, lured there by cheaper fuel for the press's steam boilers in the form of coal. "They will be greatly missed from our little burg," lamented the correspondent to the *Kalamazoo Semi-Weekly Telegraph.* The following afternoon, a fire of mysterious origins totally destroyed the vacant printing establishment as well as two nearby houses.

The Gospel Trumpet Publishing Co. moved again from Moundsville to Anderson, Indiana, prior to 1905. By the 1930's, it had gained the reputation as "the largest religious publishing plant in the United States."

In addition to a few surviving volumes, proudly bearing the imprint "Grand Junction," eagerly sought by book collectors, 131 Church of God congregations within the state and the Warner Memorial Camp at Grand Junction, currently a year-round retreat and camping center, bear witness to the saints' Michigan origins.

James D. Elderkin, Veteran of Three Wars

Maj. James D. Elderkin, veteran of three wars, in 1899.

The old drum major from Detroit felt like a boy again. The spirited Sousa marches and the martial tramp of the fellow Grand Army of the Republic delegates who thronged Buffalo's streets that August morning in 1897 made James D. Elderkin's blood race like it had when he stormed the gates of Mexico City with Capt. Ulysses Grant half a century before. Forgotten were his 76 years, his rheumatism and sore feet—white-haired head held high, he would march in the grand review, under the gigantic arch formed by the letters GAR at the corner of Main and Niagara streets, with the best of them.

Ten blocks later, he had had enough. Exhausted and wracked with stomach cramps, the old soldier limped out of the line of march and sank down on a wooden crate in a nearby store to catch his breath. Despite the pain, seated there with his head throbbing with the beat of the passing parade, a flood of memories washed over the old veteran.

The army had been his life. Following a western New York childhood, a teenage-job on the Erie Canal and a few years of wandering, he had enlisted at Schenectady at the age of 18. Soon, he found himself on a steamer en route to New Orleans, from where he would make his way to Fort Gibson, Indian Territory (now Oklahoma), to join the 4th U.S. Infantry Regiment.

There, Elderkin spent two years guarding the Cherokees and Creeks who had been removed from their ancestral lands in the Southern states. In 1841, his regiment was transferred to Florida to fight the Seminoles, a tribe that refused to comply with the government program of removal beyond the Mississippi.

Elderkin remembered hacking his way through the cypress swamps, thick with cottonmouths, rattlesnakes, alligators and poisonous insects, expecting at any time to be ambushed by the tough Seminole guerrillas. That year spent in Florida he recalled as the worst hardship he experienced in any of the three wars in which he would fight.

The soldiers managed to kill or capture the majority of

the Seminole, but they never did conquer a band of 150 that retreated into the Everglades. Not until 1934 would the Seminole War be declared officially over.

Following his tour of duty in Florida, Elderkin bounced around to various frontier posts: Fort Gibson, Jefferson Barracks near St. Louis and Fort Scott, Kansas Territory. Despite the miserable pay of $7 a month, he found the security and camaraderie of military life to his liking. He eventually parlayed his childhood fondness for playing the flute into an assignment as a musician, and he grew adept at the trumpet and trombone.

In 1846 Elderkin's unit joined Gen. Zachary Taylor's army of occupation at Corpus Christi, Texas, which was engaged in protecting the disputed territory between the Nueces and Rio Grande rivers. An attack by Mexican forces precipitated the battles of Palo Alto and Resaca de la Palma, and on May 13, 1846, the U.S. Congress declared war on Mexico.

During Taylor's ensuing campaign across the Rio Grande, Elderkin became "the first man to carry the American colors onto Mexican soil." His unit was subsequently transferred from Taylor's to Gen. Winfield Scott's command, which landed at Vera Cruz and fought its way through the Mexican interior to Mexico City.

Following the successful Battle of Chapultepec on September 13, 1847, against overwhelming odds, Scott pushed on to storm the walls of Mexico City. In intense hand-to-hand fighting, the U.S. Infantrymen hacked their way through the city.

Elderkin wounded and captured a Mexican soldier. Encountering Capt. Ulysses "Sam" Grant, who had relinquished his duties as quartermaster to see some action at the front, Elderkin asked him what he should do with his prisoner. "Break his gun and let him go," Grant grunted.

Elderkin then joined Grant and some 30 other soldiers who sallied forth along the aqueduct which supplied the city to capture a small fort. Hoisting a small cannon to the belfry of a nearby church, Grant blasted away to cover the Americans, who inched forward, fighting from house to house. The Mexicans soon surrendered the city, and for all practical purposes, the war was won.

Elderkin was to see a good deal more of Grant following the victorious Americans' return home. Both were transferred to the newly created 4th Infantry Regiment headquarters at Detroit, Elderkin as drum major of the unit band and Grant as quartermaster.

Grant and his new wife Julia took temporary lodging at the National Hotel, but by July 1849, they were comfortably situated in a cottage at 253 Fort Street East. Both soldiers found garrison duty at Detroit a welcome respite from battle. Grant amused himself with horse racing down the city streets and on the frozen River Rouge in the winter. He also enjoyed escorting his pretty young wife to the various social occasions and dances the city offered.

Grant remembered the musician he had led in battle at Mexico City, and the two struck up a friendship. Elderkin delivered Grant's mail to his home daily, and during one such walk, he noticed a beautiful dark-eyed young German girl in her yard. After that, he often brought Grant his mail twice a day. Soon, Elderkin courted Mary Bessemer, and they married.

In 1852, Elderkin was transferred to the Army garrison at Benicia near San Francisco. His wife accompanied him on the ocean voyage, which included a perilous trek across the Isthmus of Panama.

At Benicia, he again encountered Grant, who gave him a litter of pigs to feed from the garbage of the band mess hall. He raised and sold them to a local farmer at the inflated Gold Rush rate of $40 apiece. That, "thanks to my old friend, Capt. Grant," remembered Elderkin, was the first money he had managed to save during 15 years of Army life.

Soon thereafter, both Grant and Elderkin would resign from the Army. The outbreak of the Civil War, however, found Elderkin back in Detroit, where he enlisted in the 1st Michigan Infantry. Three months later, he re-enlisted in the 5th Michigan Infantry.

Grant also re-enlisted as the colonel of an Illinois regiment. During the succeeding four bloody years, his destiny was to emerge as the Union's top general and, ultimately, to serve as president of the United States.

Elderkin awoke from his revery back in the general store in Buffalo to recognize the portly figure of fellow Detroiter, Michigan Gov. Hazen Pingree, approaching. Hearing of the old veteran's distress, he had come to check on him. He supplied an ambulance to convey him back to his hotel room.

Elderkin recovered and, two years later, published in Detroit his memoirs, *Biographical Sketches and Anecdotes of a Soldier of Three Wars*.

James Corrothers,
Black Poet

James D. Corrothers posed thoughtfully for the camera in 1916.

He labored as a bootblack, waiter, porter, dockworker and other menial tasks that white society reserved for men of his color. But poverty and prejudice could not still the heart of a poet that beat within James D. Corrothers.

He was born in the famous "Chain Lake" black settlement of Calvin and Porter Townships, Cass County, on July 2, 1869. His ancestors were Zulu, Scotch-Irish, French, Malagasy and Cherokee. That made his complexion, he later quipped, "about that of the original man."

His mother died during his birth, and his father gave him up to his Scotch-Irish and Cherokee grandfather to raise. When Corrothers was two years old, the family moved further north, settling near the VanBuren County community of South Haven. That he counted as one of the lucky breaks of his life.

The only black boy attending the South Haven public schools at that time, he "grew up in an atmosphere of pure speech and enjoyed advantages of superior training" that would not have been possible had he remained in a black community. He learned to speak and act like his fellow students and differed from them only in skin color.

Like any schoolchild who is different, however, he had to prove himself. He grew adept with his fists as he thrashed nearly every white boy in town before he was finally accepted as a playmate. Because of his fighting, teachers often flogged him during his first months at school. Corrothers took his punishment stoically and studied hard. He also found the teachers "plainly interested in helping me forward," and soon he was leading most of his classes. Yet, he could never really escape the fact that he was different.

Despite its proximity to the Cass County settlement, many South Haven residents had not seen a black person before. Corrothers never forgot the time a farmer stopped him while he was walking down a country road a few miles from South Haven. "Say, little boy," he said, "just

205

you wait in the road there a minute. My little boy never saw a colored boy, and I don't want him to miss this chance." Corrothers good naturedly permitted the eight-year-old boy to investigate and to question him as to why his skin was dark.

In 1884, Corrothers and his grandfather moved to Muskegon to live with relatives. There, he found a rip-roaring lumber town whose raised wooden sidewalks, well scarred by the spiked boots of rivermen, led to scores of saloons. The city teemed with "rough men who loved big wages, red liquor, square dealing and a fight."

His school days came to an abrupt end in Muskegon. At the age of 14, he went to work in one of the many sawmills that lined Muskegon Lake, earning $4.50 for each weeks' worth of 11 hour days. He got along well with the rough, big-hearted men he worked with and found little prejudice in Muskegon. At the height of its prosperity and boasting "more money and top hats" than any other similar-sized city, Muskegon was "too busy to pay much attention to the color of a man who was a good worker and paid his bills."

But winter brought slack times to the mills. Corrothers managed to earn enough to take care of his grandfather by splitting wood at 25 cents a cord and working in a new roller-skating rink that had opened in the city. All the while, he lived a good, clean life, steered clear of liquor, eschewed dance halls and nursed a burning desire "to be somebody."

When he was 16, his grandfather went to live with relatives in Grand Rapids. Corrothers continued to eke out an existence in Muskegon until he met a Great Lakes sailor who persuaded him to stow away on a vessel headed for Chicago.

During the succeeding four years, he worked as a porter, bellhop, waiter and janitor. He spent what little spare time was allotted him in self-improvement. He read the great classics, the Bible, history and biographies of American statesmen. He particularly enjoyed poetry: Burns, Heine,

Goldsmith, Gray, Longfellow, Whittier and Tennyson.

Like many another dreamy youth, he began writing his own verse. Then, one day in 1889, just as in one of the Horatio Alger books he had read—only none of Alger's heroes were black—Corrother's got his big break. He was 19 and working as a bootblack in a fancy Chicago barber shop. As he shined the boots of a distinguished looking stranger, he began to discuss literature with him. They each quoted passages, and a friendship developed. The stranger was Henry Demarest Lloyd, social activist, writer and influential stockholder of the *Chicago Tribune*.

Corrothers gave his new friend some of his own verse to read. Ten days later, he was delighted to find one of his poems published under his name in the editorial page of the *Tribune*. Within a few months, Lloyd had also secured a job at the *Tribune* for his young protege. At $10 per week, it was the best-paying position he had ever held. Lloyd suggested he save most of his salary so he could attend college.

The position, however, was not that of a writer. Corrothers was to succeed an old black man who had served for 20 years as a porter in the *Tribune's* counting room, and, as he soon learned, that was the highest rank a black man could expect to achieve on the newspaper.

Nevertheless, Corrothers spent a month of his own time researching and writing an article about "the progress of the colored people of Chicago." The editor printed it only after he had paid another reporter to rewrite it by labeling Chicago's leading black citizens with every demeaning stereotype then in vogue. Corrothers protested and was fired. He had finally come face to face with a reality of American life—"the boding anathema of his color."

It was a bitter lesson, but it did not destroy his spirit. Corrothers returned to menial jobs, and he continued to study and to write. He gained the friendship of women's rights advocate, Frances E. Willard, and attended Northwestern University and Bennett College in Greensboro, North Carolina.

Corrothers eventually published many of his poems and essays in leading magazines and newspapers. Some were examples of the "plantation school" dialect poems that had been popularized by Paul Lawrence Dunbar. Others, such as "At the Closed Gate of Justice," expressed his outrage at the unfairness of the "color line":

"To be a Negro in a day like this
Demands forgiveness. Bruised with blow on blow,
Betrayed like him whose woe-dimmed eyes gave bliss,
Still must one succor these who brought one low,
To be a Negro in a day like this."

Corrothers ultimately became a pastor as well as a poet, successively preaching to Methodist, Baptist and Presbyterian "colored" churches in southern and eastern states. In 1907, he returned to South Haven where he constructed with his own hands the Union Baptist Church. But that community still lacked enough black residents to make it a success, and he eventually moved on to lead other flocks.

Corrothers published a collection of "Negro humor and folk lore" titled *The Black Cat Club,* in 1902. His autobiography, *In Spite of the Handicap,* an "interesting and well written human document," according to Ray Stannard Baker, appeared in 1916.

Corrothers died three years later. Robert Kerlin's *Negro Poets and Their Poems,* published in 1923, contains four of Corrothers' best-known poems.

Caroline Bartlett Crane, Municipal Housekeeper to the Nation

Caroline Bartlett (Crane), ca. 1893.

Pressing a perfumed handkerchief to her nose to mask the sickening stench, the prim fashionably-dressed matron scanned the slaughterhouse in horror. Within the decrepit weather-beaten structure, black cobwebs draped the ceiling beams and upper walls. Below, "caked blood, grime, grease, hair, mold and quite unmentionable filth covered every inch of every exposed surface." A burly butcher, busily skinning carcasses, "wiped the grease from his knife on the manure covered flanks of the cow, and when he was not using his knife held it by the blade in his mouth."

So wrote Caroline Bartlett Crane, minister, women's rights activist and civic reformer, concerning her surprise tour of inspection of the seven slaughterhouses that ringed the outskirts of Kalamazoo in 1901. Her graphic descriptions of the unsanitary conditions she discovered, including the routine slaughtering of diseased animals, nauseated local meat-eaters five years before Upton Sinclair's novel, *The Jungle*, focused national attention on the horrors of the Chicago meatpackers.

Not content with merely exposing the evils of the virtually unregulated industry, Crane led a fight in the state Legislature to remedy the situation. The passage in 1903 of the model bill she had drafted allowed Michigan municipalities to enact inspection ordinances regulating meat sold within their border and paved the way for Crane's later similar crusades on the national level.

Such accomplishments were but one aspect of the reform efforts that would win Crane fame as "municipal housekeeper to the nation."

Born on August 17, 1858, in Hudson, Wisconsin, Caroline Bartlett moved with her family to Hamilton, Illinois, when she was 14. Two years later, a stirring sermon by a visiting Unitarian preacher inspired her to set her sights on a career as a liberal minister. Family objections to so daring an occupation for a woman caused her to temporarily abandon her goal. But in 1886, following graduation from

Carthage College and subsequent employment as a reporter on several Minnesota and Wisconsin newspapers, she launched her pulpit career as minister to a Unitarian congregation in Sioux Falls, South Dakota.

Her success there led to a calling to the First Unitarian Church of Kalamazoo. A haven for spiritual non-conformists since its founding in 1857, the church plunged into a vibrant era of social reform under Crane's dynamic leadership.

Renamed the People's Church to accent its goal of being a "seven day church" administering to the entire community every day, by 1894, it had pioneered in Kalamazoo with kindergarten, the Frederick Douglass Club for local blacks, a gymnasium for working girls, manual training classes for men and a household science course for women. By the decade's end, several of those innovations had been adopted by the Kalamazoo public school system.

In 1895, the People's Church and its minister drew national attention when, during a visit to Kalamazoo, Col. Robert G. Ingersoll, the "great agnostic" who had lampooned organized religion for decades, announced that the People's Church "is the grandest thing in your state, if not in the whole United States. If there were a similar church near my home, I would join it, if its members would permit me."

Then, on New Year's Eve 1896, the organ of the People's Church boomed out the wedding march for its minister and Dr. Augustus Warren Crane, Kalamazoo's pioneer radiologist. In order to prepare for her additional duties as homemaker, Crane enrolled in her church's household science courses. Those courses sparked an interest in learning more about the origins of locally available foods, water and hygiene in general. She discovered Kalamazoo's municipal water system, sewers, meat and dairy supplies, etc., to be appallingly unsanitary.

In conjunction with the Kalamazoo Women's Civic Improvement League, which she co-founded, Crane began

211

battling for a series of remedial programs of which her expose' of local slaughterhouses proved but the opening salvo.

In May 1904, for example, she led a campaign for clean streets modeled after a successful program adopted in New York. Downtown Kalamazooans were startled by squads of white-uniformed laborers armed with shovels, brooms and carts who combated the equine pollution that littered city streets. That experiment in "municipal housekeeping" was eventually adopted as a city program. It also enhanced Crane's reputation and helped launch her national career as a much-sought-after consultant on urban sanitation.

During the period 1907 to 1916, Crane conducted investigations of sanitary and social conditions in 62 cities in 14 states. Her sanitary surveys provided detailed analyses of everything from sewage systems to conditions in schools and jails and were often used by communities as a blueprint for reform.

By the outbreak of World War I, Crane had curtailed her sanitary survey work to devote more time to her family, which had grown to include two adopted children. However, during the war, she served with distinction as president of the Michigan Women's Committee of National Defense, which coordinated home-front volunteer activities.

In 1924, Crane again drew national attention—this time as an architect. In response to Secretary of Commerce Herbert Hoover's "Better Homes in America" contest, she designed an ideal house for the typical American family of the era.

Her "Everyman's House," an unpretentious colonial-style home constructed halfway up Kalamazoo's South Westnedge Avenue Hill, was a "space-saving, step-saving, time-saving, money-saving small house" as well as one of the first to be designed specifically for the needs of the housewife. The nursery, placed adjacent the kitchen, for example, saved a mother from endlessly trudging up and down stairs.

Crane's Everyman's House took first place in the contest over more than 1,500 other entries, and in 1925, she published a book describing her revolutionary architectural concepts.

The "municipal housekeeper to the nation" who had stepped outside the bounds of her"proper sphere" to devote her life to bettering the health and welfare of fellow citizens died in Kalamazoo in 1935. A half century later she was inducted into the Michigan Women's Hall of Fame.

Ring Lardner, the Funniest Man in Niles

Ring Lardner (left) in his Great Neck, Long Island, home in 1926.

Ring Lardner did not mind keeping all the books, billing customers, trying to collect bad debts and mopping the floor, for which the Niles Gas Co. paid him $8 for a six-day work week in 1905. What the tall, handsome 20-year-old really disliked about his job was reading gas meters.

The meters were invariably located in dark basement corners, basements festooned with cobwebs and haunted by rats. Lardner hated those repulsive rodents. He later admitted, "When I entered a cellar and saw a rat reading the meter ahead of me, I accepted his reading and went on to the next house."

Actually, America owes a debt of gratitude to those rats. Had they not made Lardner's life miserable, he might have remained at the gas company or some other mundane occupation. Heretofore, he had shown little ambition in life. But thinking of those rats, he leaped at an opportunity to become a newspaper reporter, despite the fact that he had virtually no experience in writing. Over the following three decades, Lardner would parlay his new career into a reputation as one of America's most talented sports reporters and humorists.

Born in Niles on March 6, 1885, the youngest of nine children, Ringgold Wilmer Lardner enjoyed a storybook childhood. His father's forebears had immigrated to Niles from Philadelphia in 1836 and proceeded to amass a fortune through land speculation. Lardner's mother Lena, a dominant influence in the development of his character, encouraged his love for literature and music.

He grew up at the family mansion, a large Gothic Revival structure facing the St. Joseph River. Each of the three youngest Lardner children had their own Irish nursemaid. That they were tutored at home and not allowed to leave the yard unless accompanied by a servant was compensated for by the fact that the grounds surrounding their house contained a tennis court, baseball diamond and a stable of ponies and horses. Only select neighborhood chil-

215

dren were allowed in to play.

Despite his mother's encouragement in literature, Lardner was never much of a scholar. He recalled "...we had a private tutor that came to the house every morning at 9 and stayed till noon and on account of it taking him 2 and 1/2 hours to get us to stop giggling, why there was only a 1/2 hour left for work." Not surprisingly, when Lardner took his high school entrance exam at the age of 12, he flunked.

The family's clout in the community probably influenced the school superintendent to bend the rules and allow him to be admitted provisionally, but Lardner explained it differently in an autobiographical article published in1923, "What I Ought to of Learnt in High School."

It seems that the Niles High School had a football team but no football, and Lardner's aunt had bought him one. "Well the high school team could not play football without a football and they could not play football with my football unlest I played with it too, so I didn't have no trouble making the team and it was a high school team which you couldn't be on it unlest you was a high school student, so I was safe till Thanksgiving day at lease."

Lardner soon learned the ropes of how to get through high school with a minimum of studying. He had one elderly teacher for four or five classes who was "kind of hard of hearing." Lardner sat to the back of the classroom and, as he remembered, "Well when this teacher called on me I would get up and move my shapely lips like I was answering and finely I would stop and she would say very good."

Assigned the preparation of a book of 50 differen pressed wildflowers as a botany class project, Lardner and some of his classmates found themselves "26 specimens short with 2 days between us and the end of the school year and it looked like the best thing to do was get a hold of 8 pansies, 8 violets and 10 daisies and christen them angina pectoris, in loco parentis, spinal meningitis and etc." Lardner figured he got away with that trick either because the

216

teacher was in a hurry or "maybe because she was going to be the botany teacher again next year."

Despite his success in dodging learning, Lardner graduated from Niles High School at the age of 16, and he was even offered a scholarship at Olivet College. He declined that honor, however, and took jobs with a string of Chicago firms and was successively "canned" from each. Within the year, he was back at Niles working as "third assistant freight hustler" at the Michigan Central Railroad depot. He also got fired from that position "for putting a box of cheese in the through Jackson car, when common sense should have told me that it ought to go to Battle Creek."

Following a brief attempt at studying mechanical engineering at the Armour Institute in Chicago and a year or more of lolling around his parents' house unemployed, Lardner got a job with the Niles Gas Company. He escaped the rats connected with that position due to his older brother Rex's writing ability, not his own.

Rex worked as a reporter for the *Niles Daily Sun* and as a stringer for the *Kalamazoo Gazette* and the *South Bend Tribune.* Edgar Stoll, editor of the rival *South Bend Times,* paid a visit to Niles in an attempt to get Rex to join his staff. But Rex happened to be on vacation at that time, so Stoll sought out his brother to learn his whereabouts. When Lardner found out the job paid $12 per week, he decided to try it himself. "Have you ever done any newspaper work?" Stoll asked. "Yes indeed," lied Lardner, thinking about those rats, "I often help my brother."

Lardner got the job and, amazingly enough, proved an excellent reporter. Sports, baseball in particular, were his forte. He had an ear for colorful language, and he spiced his humorous accounts of life in the ballpark with actual conversations of fans and players as well as the colloquial expressions he had learned while growing up in Niles. In other words, he wrote as Midwesterners talked rather than how they were expected to talk.

He commuted on the interurban train from Niles to

217

South Bend until, in 1907, he joined the staff of the *Chicago Inter-Ocean*. Over the succeeding five years, he bounced around to a variety of other newspapers, including the *Chicago Examiner* and the *Chicago American*. He lost his job with the latter for accidentally running the obituary of the wrong man.

In 1913, Lardner began writing a popular column in the *Chicago Tribune* called "In the Wake of the News." The following year, he published in the *Saturday Evening Post* a series detailing the adventures of a semi-literate White Sox pitcher named Jack Keefe. That series launched his national reputation and was reprinted as *You Know Me, Al* in 1916.

Lardner eventually left newspaper work to concentrate on humorous fiction. Although he is best known for his baseball stories, he ultimately authored over a dozen collections of short stories, including: *How to Write Short Stories, The Love Nest and Other Stories, Round-Up* and a mad cap autobiography, *The Story of a Wonder Man*. References to his Michigan youth occur throughout his writings.

H.L. Mencken considered Lardner one of the finest American authors of his time—"no one, sober or gay, writes better," he concluded.

Tragically, Lardner died of tuberculosis at the age of 48.

Horatio
"Good Roads" Earle

*The first International Good Roads Congress held in Port Huron
on July 4, 1900. Arrow points to Horatio Earle.*

"Wagons creaking, groaning, crashing,
  Wrecks bestrewing either bank,
Jarring, jolting, jambing, dashing
This is riding on the Plank."

That is how Asa Stoddard, "the farmer poet" from Kalamazoo County's Cooper Township, described a ride on the old plank road that linked Kalamazoo and Grand Rapids. Stoddard published his verse in 1880, at a time when Michigan's notoriously rough roads were among the worst in the nation. A quarter of a century later, anyone attempting to traverse the state by road, even in one of the 3,000 horseless carriages then owned by Michiganians, could still expect up to a week of "jarring, jolting, jambing" and pushing out of mud holes.

That year, 1905, marked the birth of the State Highway Department. Its first commissioner, Horatio Sawyer Earle, led a campaign for improved highways and, in the process, well earned the title "Good Roads" Earle.

The deplorable road system Earle sought to better stemmed in part from the state's geography. Approximately one-sixth of Michigan's total area, for example, was classified as "swamp lands," ranging from marshes to "bottomless" sloughs. A good portion of the remainder of the state's terrain consisted of powdery "blow sand."

The two major arteries that snaked across the southern portion of the state in territorial days were little more than right-of-ways hacked through the woods. Harriet Martineau, an English woman who braved a stagecoach trek over the Detroit to Chicago Military Road in 1836, described how her driver often left the main-traveled route for the relatively easier going across adjacent field and forest.

Following Michigan's stormy entrance into the Union in 1837, Gov. Stevens T. Mason launched an ambitious plan of "internal improvements" to construct roads, canals and railroads. But the subsequent hard times triggered by the financial panic of 1837 soon brought those projects to a halt and nearly caused the state government to go bankrupt in the process.

The Legislature sold the Michigan Central and Michigan Southern railroads to private companies in the 1840's. Private money also financed construction of a series of plank-surfaced toll roads. Most soon deteriorated to the condition so graphically described by "the farmer poet."

With the internal-improvements fiasco fresh in their minds, the framers of the Constitution of 1850 inserted a clause forbidding the state government from "being a party to or interested in any work of internal improvement." The Constitution of 1850 reserved for townships' governments practically the entire responsibility for constructing and maintaining rural roads. County boards of supervisors could not borrow or raise by tax more than $1,000 for highway purposes without securing voter approval.

In 1859, the Legislature passed a bill allowing the state to build roads into publicly owned swamplands in order to make them more marketable. Except for those and the privately owned plank roads, all other rural thoroughfares, including the major highways, were under township authority.

Tight-fisted township boards often spared the gravel, and poor districts generally had poor roads. Few townships could afford much in the way of road-building equipment. To further complicate matters, taxpayers with little knowledge of road building were allowed to work off a portion of their "road tax."

In general, the highway system also fell victim to the rural vs.urban dichotomy. Municipalities constructed and maintained streets that terminated at their boundaries. Urban residents were not about to fund improvements to roads traveled mainly by farmers. Rural taxpayers scoffed at the idea of paying to make holiday jaunts into the country easier for city folks.

A major milestone, however, came in1883 when the Legislature passed a special act permitting six Bay County townships, Bay City and West Bay City to consolidate as a "stone road district." A one-half mill road tax levied against all taxable properties within the district funded construction of three "state roads" that linked the townships with the cities. The resulting macadamized roads, a process whereby successive layers of crushed rock were rolled to an asphalt-like hardness, served as a model for other districts. Ten years later, a new general law offered residents the option to choose a board of county road commissioners and tax county property as a whole to improve major roads.

Even more importantly, by the 1890's, the original high-wheeled "bone crusher" had evolved into the modern-style "safety bike," and the nation was experiencing a bicycling craze. Long before motorists took up the cause, bicyclists actively campaigned for better roads. The passage of the 1893 county road law, in fact, owed a great deal to the lobbying efforts of the Michigan division of the League of American Wheelmen, a bicyclist's organization formed in 1879.

That is where Earle came into the picture. Born and raised on a farm near Mt. Holly, Vermont, the 33-year-old Earle moved to Detroit in 1889. An avid bicyclist and League of American Wheelmen member, he was appointed chairman of that organization's good roads committee in 1898.

A "hustler" with a flair for showmanship, Earle held the first International Good Roads Congress at Port Huron on July 4, 1900. There, a steam engine led a "good roads train" made up of horse-drawn road graders, dump wagons, sprinklers, steam rollers and other construction equipment loaded with 2,000 delegates.

Earle won election as a state senator in 1901, and he soon authored a resolution adopted by the Legislature to investigate the subject of highway improvements. During the following two years, he kept up a relentless campaign that resulted in the construction of several "object lesson roads."

In 1903, the Legislature created a State Highway Department and named Earle director, with an annual budget of $5,000. However, Attorney General Charles Blair ruled that act unconstitutional. Two years later, Michigan voters overwhelmingly passed a referendum exempting road improvements from the prohibited list of internal improvements.

The act of June 1, 1905, reestablished the State Highway Department and created a state reward system, whereby counties and townships could recoup up to $1,000 in state funds for every mile of road constructed according to specifications. Another provision of the 1905 act called for the now-familiar motor vehicle license fees.

When Earle took office in 1905, only 245 of Michigan's estimated 68,000 miles of road were stone or macadam. Prior to the law's repeal in 1925, $25 million in state reward funds had been paid to improve 13,467 miles of Michigan roads. That year saw the first state tax on gasoline.

Earle served as State Highway Commissioner for four years. One of the highlights of his tenure was the construction of the first mile of concrete road in the nation—on Woodward Avenue, between Six and Seven Mile roads in Detroit.

Monuments erected at Mackinaw City in 1916 and at Cass City in 1917, as well as a state highway system that has become one of America's finest, honor the pioneering efforts of "Good Roads" Earle.

David Grayson's
Adventures in Friendship

President Woodrow Wilson seated to the right of his confidant,
Ray Stannard Baker, alias David Grayson.

The farmer and his teen-age son mopped their brows repeatedly as they moved slowly along the furrows, planting potatoes. It was a warm spring afternoon sometime around the turn of the century. Their farm probably lay in Ingham County, but it might have been in Shiawassee, Clinton or Eaton, all within a good day's walk of East Lansing.

A stranger with a knapsack on his back stood leaning against the wooden fence that bordered the road, watching them labor. Unseen, he heard the boy complain that they would never be able to finish the field that afternoon. "We've got to get through here today, Ben," his father replied grimly, "we're already two weeks late."

With scarcely a word of introduction, the stranger climbed over the fence, swung off his knapsack, filled an extra basket with seed potatoes from a nearby wagon and began planting alongside the boy. "How far apart you planting 'em, Ben," he asked. "About 14 inches," the boy answered in amazement.

David Grayson had just embarked on another of his adventures. While other adventurers might find satisfaction in climbing mountains or hunting wild animals, Grayson's adventures were in discovering friendship, contentment, and the goodness and decency that is in most people.

The millions of readers who shared his adventures through a long list of publications beginning in 1906 often found their own lives buoyed up by his homespun philosophy that urged enjoyment of the simple things in life that money cannot buy.

Like most of his adventures, the potato-field episode ended happily, with the planting finished on time and Grayson invited to the farmer's home, where he met a salt-of-the-earth Michigan family with whom he shared an unforgettable meal of "huge piles of new baked bread, the sweet farm butter, already delicious with the flavor of new grass, the bacon and eggs, the potatoes, the rhubarb sauce,

225

the great plates of new, hot gingerbread and at the last, the custard pie—a great wedge of it, with fresh cheese."

Grayson recounted that culinary adventure in *The Friendly Road,* first published in 1913. What his millions of readers did not know, however, was that Grayson was actually the alter ego of Ray Stannard Baker, a muckraking journalist, famous for exposing American society's injustices in a totally different manner.

Born in Lansing in 1870, Baker and his family moved to the northern Wisconsin frontier when he was five. He grew up amid wild Indians and even wilder lumberjacks. As the family wrested their farm from the wilderness, Baker learned to love the solitude of nature.

He revered his father, a Union veteran whose military experiences had left him with two mottoes to guide him through life: "Admit nothing to be hardship" and "When in doubt, charge." Despite another rather dubious saying, "The truth is that which has gotten itself believed by me," Baker's father instilled in him a love of learning which he pursued in their home library and a one-room country schoolhouse.

At the age of 15, Baker returned to Michigan to attend Michigan Agricultural College in East Lansing. There, his chief mentor, and later his father-in-law, was the famous botany professor, William J. Beal, who taught him to observe his surroundings in detail.

While expenses were ridiculously low by modern standards, no tuition was charged, for example, Baker earned his way through college literally by the sweat of his brow. He received eight cents an hour for laboring in the farm maintained by the college and taught in nearby country schools for $30 a month.

Baker secured an excellent education at MAC, but much of it was learned outside the classroom. During the 10-day vacations that occurred in May, he developed the habit of tramping the Michigan countryside. Without a penny in his pocket and armed only with a light knapsack and his wits, he set out to enjoy and observe. Many of the adventures he later recorded in a fictional mode in his David Grayson books actually occcurred during his Michigan treks.

Following graduation in 1889, Baker returned briefly to his father's Wisconsin farm before enrolling in the law school at the University of Michigan. Once there, it did not take him long to realize that law was not his true calling. He eventually dropped out of the university, but not before taking a seminar in literature taught by Professor Fred Newton Scott, who sparked in Baker an interest in journalism.

In the summer of 1892, Baker left Ann Arbor for Chicago, where he hoped to get a job with the *Chicago News Record*. But the veteran editor to whom he showed his college diploma laughed him out of the office. After many poverty-filled months, during which he worked as a newspaper stringer and in cataloging books at the Newberry Library, he finally secured a full-time position on the paper at $12 a week.

Baker specialized in reporting about the incipient labor movement, including the controversial and often bloody strikes that polarized America. In 1894, he traveled with "Coxey's Army" of unemployed in its march to Washington to promote a WPA-type program. Although that populist movement ended in fiasco when the marchers were arrested for walking on the grass in Washington, Baker's sensitive reporting launched his national reputation. As the "Gay 90's" wore on, he became more and more an advocate of the underdog in American society.

In 1898, John S. Phillips, editor of *McClure's Magazine*, recruited Baker to join the staff of that crusading journal in New York City. During the succeeding eight years, Baker wrote a series of exposes on railroad mismanagement, the black American's dilemma, spiritual unrest in society and other stirring issues. He rose to the top ranks of the so-called "muckrakers." He made his home in Lansing,

227

beginning in 1902, until 1910 when he moved to Amherst, Massachusetts.

Originally a supporter of Theodore Roosevelt, who sought to redress many of the issues the muckrakers had championed, Baker later became one of the staunchest defenders of his progressive Democratic rival, Woodrow Wilson. Baker and Wilson became close friends. During World War I, Baker roved through Europe as an agent of the State Department, sending his reports directly to the president.

Following Wilson's death, he was appointed his official biographer, and his monumental *Woodrow Wilson: Life and Letters,* which appeared in eight volumes in 1927-1939, won a Pulitzer Prize for biography.

In the meantime, amid his hectic life as a globe-trotting journalist, Baker continued to find much-needed solace in his rural walks. Beginning in 1906, when he helped launch the *American Magazine,* he published David Grayson stories based on those wanderings.

America soon grew to love Grayson, the bachelor gentleman-farmer who left a lucrative career in the city to return to nature, his best friend the Scotch preacher and the other warm-hearted characters who dwelt in the imaginary community of Hempfield.

Adventures in Contentment, published in book form in 1907, was followed by *Adventures in Friendship* in 1910. Baker wrote seven other David Grayson books prior to his death in 1946. Not until 1916, however, when several charlatans posing as David Grayson began touring the lecture circuits, did he reveal his true identity.

Grayson's home-spun stories continue to gladden the hearts of those who can find enjoyment in simple pleasures. "It is a wonderful place, the city," wrote Grayson, "but it is no place for a man to live."

A Lost Tribe of Israel in Michigan?

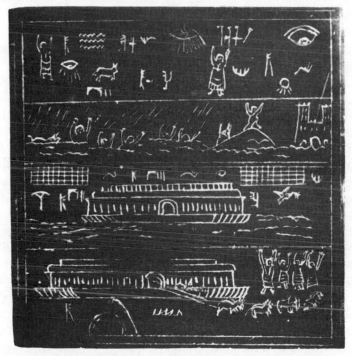

A "Soper Fraud" artifact made of black slate found in Isabella County in 1896. Note the nail-like signature in the upper right line.

Father James Savage of the Most Holy Trinity Church in Detroit pondered the significance of the wonderful artifact that had been dug up in Montcalm County's Home Township in 1907. The copper plate, coated with a green patina, bore a striking resemblance to the Ten Commandments as various artist had depicted the tablets being held by Moses. Strange engravings, an amalgam of ancient Egyptian hieroglyphics and cuneiform characters, covered the relic.

Father Savage strongly suspected that when the language experts finally cracked the code, the Michigan copper plate would be found to contain the text of the original Ten Commandments that had been handed down to Moses. His heart raced at the thought that he owned, "the greatest contribution to science and archeology that America has ever produced."

Another Detroit clergyman, Mormon Bishop Rudolph Etzenhouser, cherished similar expectations concerning the ancient Michigan artifacts he had acquired. Several of Etzenhouser's specimens were slate plates, resembling miniature tombstones, on which had been etched scenes remarkably similar to various Old Testament stories, including that of Noah and the ark. Clearly, in his eyes, these were relics of the lost tribe of Israel that had fled to North America; evidence particularly appealing to a believer in the religion that traced its origins to a set of golden plates, also artifacts of an ancient Israelite tribe, that had been translated by Joseph Smith into the *Book of Mormon*.

Nor were those learned churchmen the first to suggest that Michigan had in prehistoric days been populated by that lost tribe. M.E. Cornell, a Seventh Day Adventist minister from Battle Creek, had published, in 1892, a pamphlet about numerous clay artifacts discovered in mounds in Montcalm County. "It is quite probable," wrote Cornell, "that these mound builders were the first who found their way to this continent after the dispersion from the Tower of Babel."

The mysterious Michigan artifacts, so revered by three clergymen of rather disparate religions, had a number of things in common. First, whether the material be clay, copper or slate, all had been imprinted with a cuneiform mark resembling three upright nails, the final two crossed with another nail and followed by a leaning nail. Also, a sign painter name James O. Scotford had been involved in the unearthing and/or sale of all the artifacts. And last but not least, all the relics were "humbugs of the first water."

Michigan's famous archeological hoax, on a par with the Cardiff Giant and the Minnesota Rune Stones, has become known as the "Soper Frauds," in honor of the chief champion of the bogus artifacts, flamboyant Daniel E. Soper. His name is also perpetuated in Michigan history for his having won election as Secretary of State in 1890. But due to certain improprieties, he was forced to resign that trusted position in December 1891.

It was in 1890, also, that Scotford, purportedly, first discovered a small clay artifact while digging a post hole at his farm near the Montcalm County village of Edmore. The following spring, many other remarkable relics came to light. While excavating various nearby mounds, Scotford "manifested a skill in finding relics that made him the envy of the region." His success so inspired some residents of Stanton, the Montcalm county seat, in fact, that they organized a syndicate to acquire and exploit the artifacts. Scores of likely-looking mounds were soon ransacked. One unfortunate treasure hunter was killed when the deep, sandy hole he had excavated caved in on him.

Witnesses signed affidavits testifying that the artifacts had been unearthed at a depth of 1 1/2 to 4 feet. Most of the scores of objects, including caskets, amulets, vases, lamps, pipes and a small sphinx, were of unbaked clay. Some of the caskets also contained thin beaten-copper coins, bearing chiseled inscriptions. Curiously, the coins had a composition and weight similar to a modern copper penny.

231

Scientific analysis also revealed other suspicious facts. The clay objects contained "so large a percentage of drift sand" that they crumbled easily and dissolved in water, a trait that belied their survival underground for any length of time. The lid of one of the caskets had even been dried on a machine-sawed board.

Upon receipt of that heartbreaking scientific testimony, the Stanton syndicate disbanded operations and "pocketed its losses."

Then, in the summer of 1898, a dilapidated-looking man offered to sell the curator of the University of Michigan museum a collection of similar clay artifacts, each bearing the telltale nail-like markings. The most striking of the lot was a 21-inch-tall godlike image holding a tablet, made of baked clay. Clearly, whoever had manufactured the bogus relics had improved his technology.

When the curator pronounced the collection, which apparently had previously formed a traveling sideshow exhibit, as fraudulent, the huckster fled, leaving the treasures behind. Upon closer examination of the packing case, the curator discovered a certificate testifying that the godlike image had been unearthed near Mecosta, signed by Scotford and three others—all in the same handwriting.

By 1907, Scotford and Soper had, apparently, even further refined their art. They had also shifted operations to Detroit. Despite widespread publicity in the *Detroit News* and archeological journals concerning the "fake relic business," the charlatans found plenty of gullible buyers including Savage and Etzenhouser.

Three years later, Etzenhouser published a lavish brochure, illustrated with examples from the collection of Savage, Soper and his own, in an effort "to arouse the interests of students of philology or those engaged in historical and archeological research."

Soper continued to unearth biblical antiquities in Michigan as late as 1920. His death in 1923, however, seems to have terminated the discoveries by him or anyone else.

Heirs sold his massive collection to the University of Tulsa in 1931. University officials eventually recognized the relics for what they actually were and transferred the lot to the university theatre department for use as stage props.

Savage carried his belief in the importance of the artifacts to his death bed, at which point he willed his collection to the University of Notre Dame. That institution ultimately passed them on to the University of Utah, where they were more appreciated.

Francis W. Kelsey, a professor at the University of Michigan who for two decades led a campaign to expose the Soper frauds, summed up their final significance in an article published in 1910: "So long as human nature remains the same, it may be presumed that men will be ready to believe what they wish to believe, and that no hoax will be too preposterous to be without a following."

The Wizard of Macatawa

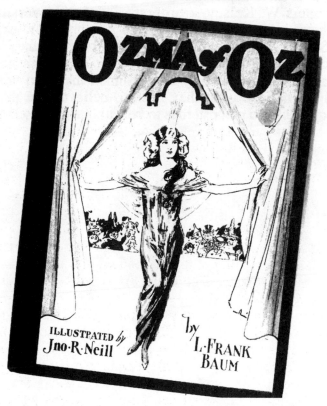

Baum wrote this sequel to the <u>Wizard of Oz</u> at Macatawa Park in 1907.

It was a pristine day in the summer of 1907, a day of golden sand, fleecy clouds in a blue sky and turquoise water twinkling with white caps. The sound of the surf and the musical cries of children at play carried up from the beach to the Queen Anne style cottages that lined the bluff at Macatawa Park, a resort community nestled at the mouth of the Black River, downstream from Holland.

On the porch of one of those cottages, a dapper, mustached, middle-aged man sat in a wicker chair softly tapping his pencil against a clipboard of typing paper that lay on his lap. He did not see the beautiful Michigan scene before him. His mind was a million miles away—in the land of Oz.

Then, L. Frank Baum began to write—to write furiously. He wrote about Dorothy Gale, a little girl from Kansas, who, while en route to Europe with her Uncle Henry, was swept overboard in a wooden chicken coop along with a talking hen named Billina. Toto stayed in Kansas with Auntie Em on this trip.

But Billina proved to be an even better companion. When their coop washed up on the beach of a strange land and they encountered the evil-tempered Nomes, the only thing that saved them was the Nomes' fear of freshly laid eggs. Dorothy also linked up with her old friends, Tin man, Scarecrow and Cowardly Lion, as well as a variety of new characters, including the benevolent and beautiful Queen of Oz, Ozma; Tiktok, the machine man; the hungry tiger and the King of Ev.

Baum published the story as *Ozma of Oz* in time for the Christmas market of 1907. It would be the second of the lavishly illustrated sequels to his 1900 classic, *The Wonderful Wizard of Oz,* that thrilled generations of American children and adults alike. Few children's books have had such an impact on American popular culture as the Oz series.

Born in Chittenango, New York, in 1846, the man who would win immortality as "the Royal Historian of Oz"

235

grew up in a wealthy, pampered environment. A congenital heart ailment prevented him from playing rough games with other children, so Baum found refuge in books, particularly romantic Victorian novels. At the age of 15, he began publishing, on his own printing press, a small newspaper called *The Rose Lawn Home Journal.*

In the 1870's and early 1880's, Baum worked as an actor and playwright. But following his marriage to Maud Gage in 1882 and the subsequent births of two sons, he was forced to leave the stage for a more lucrative livelihood. He joined the family business in Syracuse in 1886, where he sold an axle lubricant called Baum's Castorine. He also published his first book that year, a treatise on chickens.

Two years later, the Baums moved to the frontier town of Aberdeen in the Dakota Territory. There, he operated a "5 cent and 10 cent store" called Baum's Bazaar. The town's children flocked to the store to hear the fascinating stories spun by the proprietor.

But the enterprise failed to make a profit, and in 1890, Baum turned to editing the *Aberdeen Saturday Pioneer.* Until the newspaper went bankrupt the following year, Baum further honed his writing skills through a series of comical articles about local happenings. A cyclone that ripped through Aberdeen in 1890 undoubtedly inspired the twister that carried Dorothy to Munchkin Land in Baum's first Oz book.

In 1891, Baum moved his family back East to Chicago, where briefly he found employment with the *Evening Post.* Next, he tried a job as a traveling china and glassware salesman. In 1897, he returned to journalism as editor of a magazine for window dressers, *The Show Window.*

That same year, Baum published his first juvenile book, *Mother Goose in Prose,* an adaption of old nursery rhymes to contemporary themes. Its success spurred him to team up with a talented young artist, William W. Denslow, to produce a second series of fables called *Father Goose, His Book.* It became the best-selling juvenile book of 1899.

Royalties from *Father Goose* allowed the Baum family the luxury of spending the summer at Macatawa Park, a resort popular with Chicagoans. Baum first fell under the spell of the resort during a brief stay in 1899. For the next 10 season, the Baum family, which now numbered four boys, promptly left Chicago when school let out and moved to Macatawa for the entire summer.

In 1902, Baum purchased a rambling cottage there over-looking Lake Michigan. Because part of the payment came from Father Goose royalties, he named the cottage "The Sign of the Goose." Baum handcrafted oak furniture embellished with the designs of geese for the cottage. A stained-glass window featured a white goose on a green background. He also stenciled the borders of the walls with a goose motif he had designed.

At "The Sign of the Goose," Baum wrote a number of Oz books, including his first sequel published in 1904, *The Marvelous Land of Oz*. Dorothy was not a character in that book. Instead, a new creation, Professor H.M. Woggle-Bug, played a leading role. Baum got the inspiration for that character when, as he was walking the beach at Macatawa, a little girl held up a curious insect and asked Baum what it was. "A woggle-bug," he told her. Her delight with the name was second only to Baum's.

Baum wrote a poem entitled "To Macatawa" that was published in the *Grand Rapids Sunday Herald* in 1907. That same year, he wrote and privately printed, under the pseudonym John Estes Cooke, a small edition of *Tamawaca Folks*, a humorous novel that satirized life at the resort.

He also wrote 11 more books in the Oz series and more than 30 adventure novels for juveniles under such pseudonyms as Floyd Akers, Laura Bancroft, Capt. Hugh Fitzgerald, and Edith VanDyne.

But it was *The Wizard of Oz*, first published in 1900, that won Baum a permanent niche in America's heart. He based the plot on stories he had made up to entertain his own children. The word Oz came from the bottom drawer of a file cabinet labeled "O-Z."

Hailed by some critics as "the first distinctive attempt to construct a fairyland out of American materials," the volume became an immediate hit with the public and through its many editions sold millions of copies. It provided the theme for a popular stage play first produced in 1902, two silent movie versions, and the classic 1939 extravaganza starring Judy Garland. The ruby slippers, incidentally, were silver in the Baum book.

Following Baum's death in 1919, Ruth Plumley Thompson succeeded him as the Royal Historian of Oz, and for the following two decades, she produced an annual Oz book to the delight of additional generations of children each Christmas morning.

America's love affair with the land of Oz continues as strong as ever. Perhaps it is because Dorothy and her friends' odyssey in search of her home, a brain, a heart and courage holds a universal and timeless appeal. Or maybe it is because, as Baum explained, "My books are intended for all those whose hearts are young, no matter what their ages may be."

On a Train Bound for Hell: Fiery Holocaust at Metz

Twisted wreckage was all that remained following the holocaust at Nowicki's Siding.

With "a roar like a heavy thunderstorm," the wall of fire raced toward the farmhouses in Presque Isle County's Metz Township. Towering tongues of flame arched from the tree tops to ignite the fields of corn in the shock. The gale-force wind spewed sparks and whirling balls of fire onto rooftops.

It was mid-afternoon on October 15, 1908, but so dense was the smoke that it seemed as dark as night. To the German immigrant family whose farm was engulfed by the holocaust, "it did look as if the whole world was comin' to an end." Choking in the acrid smoke and rubbing their stinging eyes, the family stubbornly battled against all odds to save the farmstead they had carved from the northern wilderness.

Barefoot children scrambled across the glowing embers and firebrands that showered down. The rest of the family manned a bucket brigade to douse the walls with water and to quench the fires that broke out again and again. At the time of greatest danger, the pump handle on the well snapped off. They ripped off the cover of the well and began lowering buckets into the water with a rope.

It was about then that the train from Metz passed. Between two cars piled high with burning cedar posts and bales of tanbark was a big steel coal car filled with 50 or 60 refugees from that doomed town. The farm family heard those people "hollerin' and crying" like damned souls on a train bound for Hell.

It had been one of the strangest years for weather on record. An exceptionally warm spring and early summer with abundant rainfall had fostered a lush growth of bracken, fireweed, pokeberries and other wild vegetation. Then, July ushered in a drought. Through October, less rain fell than even during the notorious dry spells of 1871 and 1881, years that spawned forest fires which devastated millions of acres of Michigan timberland.

The once-lush ground cover lay like a bed of tinder over the land. October brought hot southerly winds which evaporated what little moisture remained in Presque Isle County, a patchwork quilt of hardwood forests, cut-over pine lands littered with brittle tree tops and branches, and tidy farmsteads peopled by German and Polish immigrants. On October 14, "the very air seemed to be charged with inflammable gases."

Yet, the approximately 200 citizens of Metz, a hodge-podge of saloons, stores, churches and residences huddled along either side of the Detroit and Mackinac Railroad tracks, seemed oblivious to the danger. The warm morning of the 15th, barefoot children clad in light summerwear padded along the dusty roads to their outlying one-room schoolhouses while their parents pursued their workday tasks. Yet, even as they did, miles to the southwest a dragon was stirring.

The actual cause of the fire remains in doubt. Some blamed sparks from a passing locomotive. Others claimed it began as a brush fire, set by land clearers, that got out of control. One thing soon became certain, however—this was no ordinary fire.

Fed by the dryness of the land and pushed on with increasing velocity by the winds that reached gale force, a sheet of fire roared across the countryside. To its rear lay blackened desolation; squarely in its path stood Metz.

By noon, residents had begun to show concern about the billowing black smoke that clouded the southwestern horizon. An hour later, they could see the glow of advancing flames and smell the smoke. Surrounded by woods and cut-over land where enormous piles of cedar posts, railroad ties and hemlock bark awaited shipment, Metz residents realized that should the fire reach their town, it was doomed.

While able-bodied men made what preparations they could to battle the approaching flames, women, children and the elderly climbed aboard a train that stood at the siding. It consisted of three cars filled with cedar posts, one with hemlock bark, and an empty steel gondola used to haul coal.

241

As Engineer William Foster awaited orders to roll, people loaded the gondola with treasured possession: trunks brought from the Old Country, bedding, ornate framed pictures of ancestors, a sewing machine... Finally, when the fire swept into a corner of the village and set a church on fire, Foster decided he could wait no longer. He chugged out of town toward Alpena with refugees packed into the gondola.

So dense was the smoke, he could hardly see. He thought the fire was behind the train, but soon, he was running through a blazing forest. As though that were not enough, the car filled with tanbark caught fire, and burning fragments began flying back onto the people in the open gondola.

Two miles southwest of Metz, at a loading point called Nowicki's Siding, great piles of hemlock bark, cedar posts and railroad ties stood along each side and close to the tracks. Foster did not realize until he had passed between the piles that they were afire. The intense heat had caused the tracks to warp, the engine derailed and the train shivered to a halt at the worst possible place.

Screaming people leaped off the gondola and ran into nearby fields. There, among the smoldering stumps, they dug away the dirt and ashes and pressed their faces into the ground. The smoke was nearly unbearable, and any exposed flesh was soon baked. Some thirty or so people remained in that position until about 3 a.m., when the flames had died down enough to allow them to drag their blistered bodies to safety. A few others had already managed to make it back to Metz, where they found little remaining but stone foundations and twisted metal.

Not so fortunate were three mothers, each with three young children, whose charred bones were found in the gondola. Escape from the locomotive, which was completely ringed by fire, had also been impossible. The brakeman succumbed as did two other passengers. Foster got badly burned before he and the fireman lowered themselves into the reserve water tank. They remained deep in water gasping for air until the heat subsided. Then, Foster made a successful dash for safety and crawled along the tracks to Posen, several miles ahead. The fireman, however, remained in the tank, until the fire burned the hose off, allowing the water to escape, and he was baked alive.

In addition to the 16 who died at Nowicki's Station, 27 others perished as the fire burned more than 200,000 acres in Presque Isle County. Hundreds of other families who had lost all earthly possessions in the fire slept outdoors that cold October night.

Despite their broken pump handle, however, the German family who had heard the awful sound of the train from Metz managed to save their farmstead. The citizens of Rogers City, Millersburg and other Presque Isle County communities also succeeded in beating back the conflagration until it died on the shores of Lake Huron.

Relief assistance flowed in from all parts of the state. The Detroit and Mackinac Railroad built shanties for the use of the homeless. Within a week after the fire, Metz boasted a temporary post office and other structures. The following spring, most of the burnt-out farmers were busy plowing their fields.

The Metz disaster is credited with influencing the state of Michigan to inaugurate its first effective forest fire protection policies.

The Nuptial Flight
of the Smiths

*Art and Aimee Smith pose beside a biplane, although not the one they
crashed in, following their wedding.*

Mrs. Preston Grandon of Hillsdale finished tying her fancy new high-button shoes and strode sedately toward the staircase. It was a Sunday afternoon in1912. Her mind set on the awaiting chicken dinner, the dignified matron had gotten about halfway down the stairs when it happened.

The heel of one of her shoes, which evidently had not been properly affixed by the manufacturer, fell off; she stumbled forward and suddenly found herself airborne. Her first solo flight ended abruptly when she crash-landed at the foot of the stairs. Although badly shaken up, fortunately, her injuries proved slight. Nevertheless, small town newspapers being what they were, her mishap made page three of the *Hillsdale Daily* on October 28, 1912.

Actually, Mrs. Grandon's plummet had been eclipsed by another that not only captured the headlines of that issue of the paper but made flying history—the world's first aerial elopement.

Art Smith, a 20-year-old stunt pilot from Fort Wayne, Indiana, employed by the Chicago-based Mills Exhibition Co., yearned to do something that no other aviator had ever done. Heretofore, however, about the only record he had achieved was for the number of times he had crashed. He wrecked so many airplanes in 1912, in fact, his colleagues nicknamed him the "Smashup Kid."

Quite naturally, the parents of his 19-year-old, pretty and fashionably plump girlfriend, Aimee Cour, also of Fort Wayne, did not think much of her cavorting around the skies with the Smashup Kid. In fact, they disapproved of the whole relationship—he seemed too, well, flighty.

Then Smith got a brainstorm. Why not spirit Aimee away in his airship and, in the process, make aviation history with the world's first aerial elopement? "Honeybug," as Smith called her, was game, and the two set October 26, 1912, as the day they would fly the coop, so to speak.

Smith's "aeroplane," patterned after the pusher-type biplane that had been invented by Glenn Curtis in 1908, was primitive by modern standards. There was no fuselage to speak of, simply a framework of pipe and steel wires with a seat and steering wheel at the front. Two feet behind the pilot's head was a big radiator that cooled the engine. The wings were of varnished silk stretched over a framework of spruce. A propeller to their rear pushed the machine forward. Obviously, the science of aviation was still in swaddling clothes, technology having improved but slightly since Orville Wright's first successful flight on December 17, 1903.

In an attempt to promote the sale of the biplanes it manufactured, the Mills Co. staged airshows throughout the Midwest. Smith had flown at one held in Hillsdale the previous June, and he evidently liked the lay of the land. In any event, he chose that community of 5,000 as the destination of his nuptial flight.

About noon on the big day, Smith started his engine and strapped himself into the pilot's seat as his honeybug squeezed in behind him. A local photographer recorded the event for posterity and the biplane taxied along the field at the outskirts of Fort Wayne (runways were yet to be invented) and slowly lifted off.

Smith planned on following the tracks of the Lake Shore Railroad to Hillsdale. But as he neared Hunterton, about 10 miles north of Fort Wayne, he developed engine trouble. He managed to land unscathed and found the engine had a broken valve. Smith dispatched a telegram to his best friend and "mechanician," Al Wertman, who soon arrived to help him replace the valve. By 3 o'clock, they were airborne once again.

Smith soared to an elevation of 1,500 feet. The telegraph operators at the 10 railroad stations along the route reported to each other the exact times the biplane passed overhead. The couple made the final 55 miles in exactly one hour—nearly a mile a minute, they marveled.

During the flight, however, Smith and his fiancee were not exactly having a lark. Her head was jammed against the sharp fins of the radiator, and in their cramped, exposed positions, both were numb from the cold wind. But the worse was yet to come.

As the plane neared Hillsdale, the engine began to misfire—then it conked out completely. Smith attempted to glide to the designated landing field, where a party of well-wishers waved in excitement. Probably due to the fact that his hands and feet were numb from the cold, he tilted the nose of the plane down too sharply, and the machine plummeted to the ground.

The airplane's nose plunged into the soft ground of a cornfield just short of the landing field, and the plane flipped over. Both passengers were thrown free.

The spectators rushed to the crash site to find the Smashup Kid nearly buried in the loose soil and his betrothed lying unconscious 15 feet away. Members of the large crowd that collected placed the two on a mattress and wiped the blood from their faces. Smith's first words when he gained consciousness were "How's Aimee?" As soon as she came to, she asked, "How's Art?" Both suffered cuts and bruises and wrenched backs but, fortunately, no serious injuries.

Transported to a nearby hotel where they were laid out in adjoining rooms, both shook from head to foot from the cold and trauma of the crash for several hours. All the while, Smith pleaded to be allowed to see "his poor little girl." Finally, he declared, "We are going to be married tonight, anyway."

The couple hoped that an Episcopal minister, the Rev. W.F. Jerome, might perform the ceremony, but he, they discovered, was addressing a women's suffrage meeting in nearby Litchfield that night. They were able to secure a substitute, the Rev. C.E. Thomas. At 11 that night, as they lay together on "a bed of pain," he united the Smiths as man and wife.

When the bride's parents learned of the marriage the next morning, they "wired their forgiveness to the happy

247

couple but urged them to return by train and leave their former means of travel" in Hillsdale. Several days later, the honeymooners took that advice.

Smith went on to carve out another aeronautical niche for himself as one of America's pioneer airmail pilots.

His bride, however, told a *Hillsdale Daily* reporter before she left town that "I am not the least bit afraid to fly with Art, but do not expect to do so again." Perhaps that is why their marriage ended in divorce two years later.

The Big Blow of 1913

The Isaac M. Scott and all hands went to the bottom of Lake Huron during the Big Blow of 1913.

Salty old Capt. George Holdridge, veteran of years of sailing the China Sea, nervously tapped the barometer as his steamer, the Robert W. Bunsen, plowed through the placid waters of Lake Huron. It was Friday, November 7, 1913, a beautiful but eerie day. The temperature stood at a balmy 80 degrees and "the sky had an odd, coppery hue that reflected on the water and gave everything an unreal appearance."

About noon on that day, as his vessel passed Harbor Beach on the east coast of the thumb, he turned to his second mate, shook his head ominously and exclaimed, "Boy, you're going to see a storm such as you never saw before!"

The old captain knew his stuff. The nightmare of shrieking wind and monster waves that struck the Great Lakes that weekend would be the worst in recorded history. The Bunsen made the sanctuary of the Detroit River, but even as it did, shipmasters less wise would disregard U.S. Weather Bureau warnings and head up the lake. For some, it would be their last voyage.

November has traditionally been a hazardous month for Great Lakes shipping. Sudden violent storms, coupled with unusual risks taken by ship owners eager to make as many voyages as possible before winter's ice closed the Sault Canal and the Straits of Mackinac, have sent many a proud vessel to the bottom.

The storm that would become known as "The Big Blow" had its origins in a huge low-pressure area that roared east from the Aleutians across Canada. It collided over Lake Superior with another low-pressure system that had arched northward from the Rocky Mountains. Together, they spawned a hurricane-strength blizzard. As the storm raged across Lake Superior then south, it met a third low-pressure front that had moved north in an abnormal pattern from the Gulf of Mexico.

A savage blizzard paralyzed cities from Chicago eastward. Freezing rain toppled trees and powerlines, and two feet of snowfall created 5- to 8-foot drifts. But the thousands marooned in their homes without electricity or telephone for three or four days were fortunate indeed compared to the sailors who faced the furious winds and waves out on the big lakes.

The steamer L.C. Waldo, loaded with iron ore, was halfway across Lake Superior when the storm struck early in the morning of November 8. Huge waves tossed the heavy ship about like a cork. Suddenly, Capt. John Duddleston heard a tremendous roaring noise. He shouted into the ship's telephone, "By God, stand by for a big one. Here it comes!" The crest of the giant wave broke over the ship mast-high, as tons of green water thundered down over its deck. Duddleston and his first mate dove into a hatchway as the wave swept the pilot house completely off the deck.

Somehow, they managed to crawl to the forward deck house where, with a hand compass from one of the lifeboats, Duddleston tried to navigate the big ship toward the shelter of Manitou Island off the tip of the Keweenaw Peninsula. He almost made it, but the hurricane-force wind drove the vessel onto the rocky shore, and the ship broke in two.

Fortunately, the bow that clung to the rocks remained above the water. The 27 men and 2 women aboard huddled in the forepeak without blankets and with only two cans of food. They managed to build a fire in a bathtub and burned the room's wooden paneling and anything else combustible. Miraculously, they held out for three days until, during a daring rescue attempt by U.S. Lifesaving Service boats from Eagle Harbor and Portage Lake, all were saved.

The crews of the Leafield and the Henry B. Smith, which sank in Lake Superior, however, were not so fortunate. None of the 43 men aboard survived the storm.

Lake Huron received the full brunt of the storm from the north on Sunday. Then, the blizzard from the south roared in to create a cyclone of savage intensity. Winds reached 90

251

mph, whipping waves that towered 40 feet from trough to crest. Worse yet, veteran seamen who had never seen the like found their vessels battered by giant waves from one direction while 80-90 mph gusts of wind struck from another. Meanwhile, an unrelenting snowfall obliterated visibility.

The storm rage unabated for 24 hours. Fortunate indeed were those ships that merely ran aground or were cast up on the rocks. Their crews had a chance of survival. But not one of the 178 sailors aboard the eight ships that sank lived to tell his story.

The exact fate of only one of those eight vessels is known for sure. Capt. Walter Iler of the George G. Crawford watched in horror as the 436-foot Argus, loaded with coal, was lifted by one huge wave on the bow and another on the stern. That left the midsection supported by nothing but air. Iler later reported, "The Argus just appeared to crumple like an eggshell and then disappeared."

The storm began to abate on Monday. That morning, Capt. George Plough, commander of the life saving station at Port Huron, spied a "dark object, about 100 feet long and quite wide," floating about three miles offshore. It proved to be the overturned hull of a big freighter. Since the bow and most of its length were under water, it was impossible to determine what ship it was. The identity of the mystery ship remained in question for four days until a diver descended to discover that it was the 524-foot ore carrier, the Charles S. Price.

Never before in the history of Great Lakes shipping had a loaded ore carrier capsized. The mystery of the sinking of the Price did not end there, either. When the bodies of some of the Price's crew began washing ashore across the lake on the Canadian side, they were found to have on life preservers from another vessel, the 269-foot Regina. Some of the bodies of the Regina's sailors who also washed ashore had on life preservers from the Price. In one case, bodies from both vessels were found entwined in each other's arms.

What actually happened to the two vessels during that terrible storm will probably never be known. The most probable explanation is that they collided, and sailors jumped from one to the other before they both went down.

The other vessels that went to the bottom of Lake Huron during the storm were the 524-foot Isaac M. Scott, the 550-foot James Carruthers, the Wexford, the John A. McGean and the Hydrus.

Lake Michigan and Lake Erie also each claimed a ship and all aboard. That brought the storm's total to 12 ships sunk, 25 ships driven ashore and anywhere from 250 to 300 sailors drowned.

The big blow of November 1913 remains the worst storm in the history of the Great Lakes.

Red Arrow Men
in World War I

"Red Arrow" Division soldiers in France during World War I. Black members of the group were restricted to non-combat roles such as truck driver and cook.

O ver the top into "no-man's land" the men of the 126th Infantry, 32nd Division, raced. Into the hell of shell-crater pocked mud, mustard gas, tangled barbed wire and whistling, shrieking leaden messengers of death they stumbled during the pre-dawn hours of August 1, 1918.

For those Michigan doughboys, the long wait was over. Forgotten was the tiresome garrison duty on the Mexican border during Gen. "Blackjack" Pershing's pursuit of Poncho Villa in 1916 and the interminable drilling at Camp Grayling and Camp MacArthur, Waco, Texas. Forgotten were the tearful goodbyes and cheering hometown throngs that regaled the troop trains, the threat of submarine attack during the tense two-week voyage to France in February 1918 and the humiliating first five months "Over There" when the division had been broken up and assigned to mundane supply duty. Forgotten also, was the gnawing dread felt by many a young man imbued with more patriotism than wisdom that the war would end before he got into actual combat.

Finally, they would earn that coveted combat experience—against battle-hardened German divisions. By evening, one out of every five of the Michigan men would lie dead or wounded, and the rest would never see the world in quite the same way again.

Campaigning under the slogan, "He kept us out of war," President Woodrow Wilson had won re-election in1916. But Germany's unrestricted submarine warfare, which sank American vessels, inexorably drew the United States into the conflict that had ravaged Europe since 1914. On April 6, 1917, Congress declared war against Germany.

America entered the war when the Allied effort was at a low point. Although it would be many months before appreciable numbers of American combat troops fought alongside the French and British, U.S. money, material and munitions helped restore Allied morale.

The American army, which numbered only 200,000 men

when war was declared, would expand more than twenty-fold, and over two million soldiers would arrive in France by the war's end in November 1918.

Of the 42 American divisions that went to war, none had more esprit de corps than the 32nd "Red Arrow" Division, composed of Michigan and Wisconsin National Guard units. Its 126th Infantry Regiment, made up almost entirely of Michigan men, was commanded by career soldier Col. Joseph B. Westnedge of Kalamazoo.

A massive offensive launched in the spring of 1918 by German Gen. Erich von Ludendorff had pushed a bulge in the German lines to within 50 miles of Paris by mid-July. On July 18, Gen. Ferdinand Foch, supreme commander of the western front, began a counter-attack known as the Aisne-Marne Offensive. Approximately 270,000 American troops would participate in the campaign.

The 126th Infantry moved into the front line along the Ourcq River on July 30th. The following day, it advanced northeast under intense German artillery fire toward its objectives, the village of Cierges and a densely forested region known as the Jomblets Woods. After digging in for the night, at 3:30 the next morning, the Michigan infantrymen went over the top to first meet Germans in combat. Soon, elements of the 126th Infantry were engaging enemy soldiers entrenched at the border of the Jomblets Woods in intense hand-to-hand fighting.

Sgt. Dougald Ferguson of Grand Rapids was leading his machine gun squad in the attack when they found themselves being raked by a machine gun nest directly to their front. The German "Maxim-type" machine gun was much more effective than the Hotchkiss gun, which was prone to jam, and the inaccurate French "Chau-chat" automatic rifles that were, at that time, both standard issue to American troops. The superior Browning water-cooled machine gun would not become available to American troops until the war was nearly over.

As bullets whined and thudded around them, Ferguson's

men could do little but press themselves as flat as they could against the mud. To attempt to charge the chattering machine gun would have been suicidal. But Ferguson managed to crawl to one side, and he eventually got behind the German emplacement. Rushing the position, he shot one of the gunners, bayoneted the other two and returned to his squad carrying the German machine gun. He was awarded the Distinguished Service Cross for his bravery.

The 500 yards the 126th had taken by nightfall proved of strategic importance. The Germans were forced to withdraw. However, 82 men of the 126th died and 378 more were wounded during the day's engagement. Men of the other Red Arrow units also performed many other acts of heroism during the succeeding campaign, fighting with such savagery that a French general nicknamed them "Les Terribles."

By August 6, the Aisne-Marne Offensive had resulted in an Allied victory, with the German bulge pushed back to a line that stretched from Soissons to Reims. Throughout the remainder of the war, which officially ended November 11, 1918, the 32nd Division continued to serve as one of the elite "shock divisions" that were hurled against the enemy "every time the Huns became obstinate and refused to budge from their stronghold, to pry them loose from their positions and give them a head start toward the Rhine."

Following the armistice, the 32nd served on occupation duty in Germany. Transported back home in May 1919, the returning heroes were greeted with parades in Detroit, Grand Rapids, Port Huron, Kalamazoo and other "home towns."

Sadly, the 126th Regiment's beloved Col. "Joe" Westnedge had died of pneumonia on November 9, 1918. Kalamazoo townspeople renamed West Street in his memory. Southwestern Michigan's Red Arrow Highway also honors the division that fought so gallantly in the "war to end all wars."

Thomas E. Dewey, Attorney for the People

Thomas E. Dewey and family posed for a campaign photo in 1944.

Young Lancelot rode out of the west—Owosso, Michigan, to be exact—to give battle to the forces of evil that held New York City in their grip. Twenty-eight year old Thomas E. Dewey, prosecuting attorney par excellence, would successfully joust with the likes of Luckie Luciano, Legs Diamond, Dutch Shultz, Waxie Gordon and a host of the other mobsters, racketeers and underworld vermin who paved a bloody path to power during the "bad old days" of the 1930's.

Over the course of his crusade for justice, during which he rose to the rank of New York County District Attorney and laid the groundwork for a state and national political career, Dewey put behind bars an amazing 72 out of 73 defendants. Income tax evasion became the sword in his strong right hand with which he toppled gangsters from their thrones.

Illicit beer baron Irving Wexler, alias Waxie Gordon, became, in 1933, the first top-rank criminal to be felled by Dewey. Ironically, Gordon's conviction came five days before Prohibition ended, thus making beer drinking legal once more.

Next came lightning raids on prostitution rings, a network of loan sharks, a marriage license shakedown run by a clerk of the city marriage bureau and a Sicilian "artichoke king" who had through intimidation and violence cornered the market on those vegetable delicacies.

Fowlest of the rackets exposed by Dewey, however, was the gigantic poultry ring headed by Tootsie Herbert. Herbert, a "slim, slick-haired" former dance-hall bouncer who had earned his nickname through his generous use of sweet-smelling colognes and hair tonics, had browbeaten his way into a position as a delegate for the New York Chicken Truckers Union, Local 167 in 1923. Through the use of strong-arm tactics, he soon rose to the top of the pecking order and had himself elected union boss for life.

Soon, Herbert egged on his trusty confederate, a former safecracker named Joe Wiener, to infiltrate the Orthodox

Jewish Chicken Killers' or Shochtim Union. Then, the two began plucking consumers and feathering their own nests. They levied an extortion fee of one cent per pound on the majority of the 200 million pounds of fowl sold in the city annually. Those who refused to comply had their trucks bombed and chicken coops burned.

Every scoop of chopped liver, every bite of chicken a al king, every turkey drumstick, every gulp of chicken soup spooned by a loving mother to the invalid's waiting mouth paid a tribute to Wiener and Herbert. Not content with that, the weasels monopolized the grain business. Next, only chicken crates rented at their exorbitant rates could convey birds into the city. The poultry racketeers' take reached nearly $50 million. In the 1930's, that was no chicken feed.

But in 1937, Dewey and a small army of lawyers, accountants and special investigators raided the illicit henhouse. Herbert was speedily toppled from his perch and sentenced to a 10-year stay in a steel-barred coop at taxpayer's expense.

Dewey's amazing string of victories over the racketeers won him national fame as "attorney for the people." Poets chanted his praise:

"Let Dewey do it! And Dewey did.
Dewey's magic was simply that
He did the job he was working at!
But do we duly do honor to
The work of Dewey? We do! We do!"

Born in Owosso on March 24, 1902, Dewey was descended from a long line of newspaper editors. His paternal grandfather, George Martin Dewey, one of the founders of the Republican Party "under the oaks" in Jackson in 1854, had edited newspapers in Hastings and Niles before moving to Owosso, where he established the *Times*. Dewey's father, George Martin Dewey, Jr., took over that editorship following his father's death. He also served as Owosso postmaster.

Dewey enjoyed a happy childhood in Owosso, playing along the Shiawassee River which meanders through the city. He worked as a newspaperboy and on local farms, saving up $800 by the time he was 17, through which he financed his four years at the University of Michigan. While in Ann Arbor, he wrote for the *Michigan Union* and took up the formal study of singing. He starred in an annual college opera and won first prize in a Michigan State Singing Contest.

Following graduation, he continued his voice lessons at the Chicago Musical College. There, he met and fell in love with Frances Hutt, a beautiful young mezzo-soprano. Meanwhile, Dewey had decided to pursue a career in law. His first choice, Harvard, however, refused to accept credits from the U-M.

When Hutt returned to New York to continue her musical training, Dewey enrolled in Columbia Law School so as to be near his fiancee. He also took additional voice lessons in New York until his teacher advised him that his singing lacked the emotion that would bring him outstanding success.

After graduation from Columbia in 1925, Dewey took a bicycle tour of Europe before settling down to a position with a New York law firm. His brilliant trial work brought him to the attention of George Z. Medalie, U.S. attorney for the Southern District of New York, who hired the 28-year-old as his assistant. Thus began Dewey's campaign against the "big apple's" mobsters, racketeers and other bad birds.

The fame he won through his bulldog tenacity inspired him to run for governor of New York in 1938. He lost that race in a close decision but ran again in 1942, winning by a large margin. Against his better judgement, he accepted the GOP presidential nomination in 1944, waging a spirited but hopeless race against President Franklin Roosevelt.

Nominated again in 1948 to run against President Harry Truman, Dewey seemed to all poll-takers a shoo-in. And much to Truman's glee, the *Chicago Tribune's* first edition headlines erroneously named Dewey the victor.

Although Dewey announced he would never run for public office again, he later recanted and ran successfully for a third term as governor in 1950. Returning to private practice in 1955, Dewey continued his powerful behind-the-scenes influence in the Republican Party. He occasionally visited his home town, where the "also ran" remained a "favorite son."

Dewey died in 1971 at the age of 68.

When Michigan's History Went Up in Smoke

Smoke swirls around his ankles as Gov. G. Mennen Williams (left) tours the burning State Office Building on February 8, 1951.

Richard C. Shay was desperate. The 19-year-old State Highway Department employee had received a letter from the Ingham County Draft Board ordering him to report for a pre-induction physical. It was Thursday, February 8, 1951—U.S. ground forces were battling communists in North Korea. Shay's fellow workers had told him "he would be in the trenches in a couple of months." He could not bear the thought of leaving his pretty 18-year-old wife and 7-month-old daughter for two years—or maybe forever.

One of the questions on the draft form he had received kept going through his mind. It had asked if he had ever been arrested or placed on probation. Shay decided to commit a trivial offense, confess to it and then, he hoped, be placed on probation—that would keep him out of the Army.

At 11:42 a.m., Shay got up from his desk in the Highway Department microfilm room located in the mezzanine between the sixth and seventh floors of the State Office Building at 300 S. Walnut Street in downtown Lansing. He struck a match, lit his pipe then calmly held the flame to the corner of one of the maps that littered the room. Then, he closed the door to the room and joined 1,300 state employees who were streaming out of the building for their lunch break. Shay drove to the trailer he lived in and ate a meal with his wife.

At 12:40, Rogna Eustis, who had returned to her work station on the seventh floor, smelled smoke. She quickly pulled a fire alarm box in the hall. Within three minutes, five fire trucks and 50 firemen had raced to the scene. When Capt. Robert Foster, the first to arrive, tried to enter the mezzanine floor, a blast of heat and smoke drove him back, and he fell to the floor unconscious.

An eight-story horseshoe-shaped structure that sprawled over most of an entire city block, the State Office Building had been constructed of reinforced concrete and marble in 1919 through 1922. Highly touted for its fireproof quali-

264

ties, the structure housed various state agencies and the 500,000 volume State of Michigan Library. Much of the vault-like mezzanine floor served as a storage area for irreplaceable state records dating back to territorial days, including all the historical documents that had been collected by the Michigan Pioneer Society in the 19th century.

Fed by those tons of paper and microfilm, the conflagration spread rapidly over the mezzanine and seventh floor. Heavy black smoke billowed from the roof. The intense heat and smoke drove the firefighters back. They hoisted an aerial ladder in the rear courtyard and began pouring 750 gallons of water a minute onto the blaze. But the oven-like structure defied all efforts to break through, and the flames continued to spread.

A plan to dynamite a hole in the mezzanine floor was abandoned because the heavy charge necessary might collapse the entire structure and damage nearby buildings. Firemen began cutting a hole in the sixth floor ceiling with air hammers, but they were stopped by steel girders.

Gov. G. Mennen "Soapy" Williams donned boots and made an inspection tour all the way to the seventh floor, where he encountered smoke "so thick it could have been cut with a knife." Fearful of his safety, firemen asked the intrepid governor to leave.

That evening, orange flames burst through the seventh floor windows. The Lansing Fire Department requested assistance from other cities. By early morning, additional ladder trucks and pumpers had arrived from Battle Creek, Flint and Grand Rapids. Local construction companies provided three tall booms on which were mounted hoses. Approximately 5,000 gallons of water a minute were being poured onto the inferno.

Rivers of water cascaded down stairwells and through the ceilings. Volunteers scoured the city for tarps to protect the books, records and equipment in the floors below. The temperature dropped to 10 degrees below zero that night, and huge stalactites of ice draped the building's exterior.

265

The fire continued to rage all day Friday. The mezzanine ceiling collapsed, and a 72-ton telephone switchboard on the seventh floor crashed through. Fifteen fire fighters were injured by falling debris or smoke inhalation. Miraculously, no one was killed.

By Saturday morning, the 25 million gallons of water that had been hosed into the building had smothered the flames enough to permit an inspection tour. Practically all of the valuable records, historical collections and manuscripts on the top two floors of the structure lay in charred heaps.

Still, the fire continued to smolder—not until February 17 was it officially declared out. In the meantime, Shay had confessed. Arraigned on February 19, he pleaded guilty to arson. The incendiary draft dodger escaped Korea but spent a tour of duty in a state institution. Ironically, Shay later worked as a hod-carrier during the construction of the new State Records Center built on North Logan Street.

The fire had caused an estimated $7 million in damage. The top two stories of the structure were completely ruined and were removed during the rebuilding process. Renamed the Cass Building, the structure continues to house state offices.

The disaster was branded "one of the greatest library catastrophes in American history." The state's historical holdings were particularly hard hit. The only group of archival records that survived were a series of incoming correspondence to the executive branch.

State Library personnel began moving tons of water-logged and frozen books on February 14. State Librarian, Loleta Fyan, established a salvage center at the Boy's Vocational School Field House. There, over a three-week period, 50,000 books were painstakingly laid out on the bleachers to dry.

The final tally revealed that 43,000 volumes had been destroyed, including unique state documents, newspapers, periodicals and rare editions. Another 19,000 partially soaked books were rebound. Among the damaged items was a folio set of Audubon's hand-colored engravings worth tens of thousands of dollars.

The State Library was relocated to a decrepit office building on Shiawassee Street and later to an old warehouse on Michigan Avenue. During the following four decades, librarians, archivists and historians campaigned for better facilities. Finally, the Michigan Library and Historical Center, which opened in 1989, was constructed at a cost of $36 million as a permanent home for our state's precious historical heritage.

BIBLIOGRAPHY

1. Father Marquette

Donnelly, Joseph P. *Jacques Marquette, S.J.* Chicago, 1968.

May, George S., ed. "The Mission of St. Ignace and Father Marquette," *Michigan History.* Vol. 42, No. 3 (September 1958) p. 257-287.

Shea, John Gilmary. *Discovery and Exploration of the Mississippi Valley: With the Original Narratives of Marquette...* N.Y., 1852.

Steck, Francis Borgia. *Marquette Legends.* N.Y., [1960].

Thwaites, Reuben G. *Father Marquette.* N.Y., 1902.

2. Chief Pontiac

Catlin, George B. *The Story of Detroit.* Detroit, 1926

[Navarre, Robert]. *Journal of Pontiac's Conspiracy 1763.* [Detroit, 1912].

Peckham, Howard H. *Pontiac and the Indian Uprising.* Princeton, N.J., 1947.

3. Charles de Langlade

Freeman, Douglas Southall. *George Washington: A Biography; Young Washington.* Vol. 2. N.Y., 1948.

Lawson, Publius V. *Bravest of the Brave: Captain Charles de Langlade.* [Menasha, Wisc., 1904].

Story, Noah. *The Oxford Companion to Canadian History and Literature.* Toronto, 1967.

Thwaites, Reuben G., ed. "Augustin Grignon's Recollections," *Collections of the State Historical Society of Wisconsin.* Vol. III (1857).

Wilson, James Grant & Fiske, John. *Appletons' Cyclopedia of American Biography.* 6 Vols. N.Y., 1888.

4. Gnadenhutten

Burton, Clarence M. "The Moravians at Detroit," *Michigan Pioneer Collections.* Vol. 30 (1905). p. 51.

Day, John E. "The Moravians in Michigan," *Michigan Pioneer Collections.* Vol. 30 (1905). p 44.

DeSchweinitz, Edmund. *The Life and Times of David Zeisberger.* Philadelphia, 1870.

Jackson, Helen Hunt. *A Century of Dishonor.* Boston, 1885.

The Ohio Guide. N.Y., (1940).

Rondthaler, Edward. *Life of John Heckewelder.* Philadelphia, 1847.

5. River Raisin Massacre

Brown, Samuel R. *An Authentic History of the Second War for Independence.* 2 Vols. Auburn, N.Y.,1815.

Darnell, Elias. *A Journal Containing an Accurate and Interesting Account...of Those Heroic Kentucky Volunteers and Regulars Commanded by General Winchester in the Years 1812-1813...* Philadelphia, 1854.

Gilpin, Alec R. *The War of 1812 In the Old Northwest.* East Lansing, 1958.

Hamil, Fred C. *Michigan In the War of 1812.* John M. Munson Fund Pamphlet No. 4. Lansing, 1960.

Tucker, Glen. *Poltroons and Patriots.* 2 Vols. Indianapolis, [1945].

6. Walk-in-the-Water

Bowen, Dana Thomas. *Lore of the Lakes.* Daytona Beach, Fla., 1940.

Catlin: *Story of Detroit.*

Farmer, Silas. *The History of Detroit and Michigan.* 2nd ed. 2 Vols. Detroit, 1889.

Hatcher, Harlan. *Lake Erie.* Indianapolis, [1945].

[Mansfield, J.B.], ed. *History of the Great Lakes.* 2 Vols. Chicago, 1899.

Mills, James C. *Our Inland Seas.* Chicago, 1910.

Quaife, Milo. *Lake Michigan.* Indianapolis, [1944].

Trowbridge, Charles C. "Detroit, Past and Present," *Michigan Pioneer Collections.* Vol. 1 (1877). p. 371.

7. Gurdon Hubbard

Dunbar, Willis F. *Kalamazoo and How It Grew.* Kalamazoo, 1959.

Hubbard, Gurdon Saltonstall. *Autobiography of.* Chicago, 1911.

Kyes, Alice Prescott. *Romance of Muskegon.* Muskegon, 1974.

8. Grand Island

Castle, Beatrice Hanscom. *The Grand Island Story.* Marquette, 1974.

Copway, George. *The Life, History and Travels of Kah-Ge-Ga-Gah-Bowh...* Philadelphia, 1847.

Grand Island Park, Lake Superior. Negaunee, [ca. 1904].

Hoogterp, Edward. "Going Public," *Kalamazoo Gazette.* 13 August 1989.

Rawson, A.L. "Pictured Rocks of Lake Superior," *Harper's New Monthly Magazine.* No. CCIV (May 1867). p. 681.

Royce, Charles C. "Indian Land Cessions in the United States," *18th Annual Report of the Bureau of American Ethnology.* Part 2. Washington, 1899.

Schoolcraft, Henry Rowe. *Narrative Journal of Travels...* Albany, 1821.

9. Drummond Island

Bigsby, John J. *The Shoe and Canoe or Pictures of Travel in the Canadas.* 2 Vols. London, 1850.

Cook, Samuel F. *Drummond Island: The Story of the British Occupation 1815-1828.* Lansing, 1896.

Quaife, Milo M. and Bayliss, Joseph and Estelle. *River of Destiny: The St. Marys.* Detroit, 1955.

10. Erie Canal

Andrist, Ralph K. "The Erie Canal Passed This Way," *American Heritage.* Vol. XIX, No. 6 (Oct. 1968). p. 22.

Colden, Cadwallader D. *Memoir...At the Celebration of the Completion of the New York Canals.* N.Y., 1825.

Hayne, Coe. "Leonard Slater—Who Gave His Youth," *Michigan History.* Vol. 28, No. 3 (July-Sept. 1944). p. 390.

Mason, Philip P., ed. "Rochester to Mackinac Island, 1830," *Michigan History.* Vol. XXXVII, No. 1 (1953). p.

27.

Merrill, Arch. *The Towpath*. Rochester, N.Y., [1954].

Shaw, Ronald, "Michigan Influences Upon the Formative Years of the Erie Canal," *Michigan History*. Vol. XXXVII, No. 1 (1953). p. 1.

11. Waukazoo

Blackbird, Andrew. *History of the Ottawa and Chippewa Indians of Michigan...* Ypsilanti, 1887.

Leelanau Township Historical Writers Group. *A History of Leelanau Township*. (Chelsea, 1983).

Littlejohn, Flavius J. *Legends of Michigan and the Old North West*. Allegan, 1875.

Lorenz, Charles J. *The Early History of Saugatuck and Singapore, Michigan 1830-1840*. [Saugatuck, 1983].

_____. "The Early History of the Black Lake Region—1835-1850." Unpublished manuscript.

VanReken, Donald L. *Ottawa Beach and Waukazoo a History*. [Holland, 1987].

12. John Ball

Baxter, Albert. *History of the City of Grand Rapids*. N.Y., 1891.

Everett, Franklin. *Memorials of the Grand River Valley*. Chicago, 1878.

Powers, Kate Ball, Hopkins, Flora Ball and Ball, Lucy, compilers. *Autobiography of John Ball*. Grand Rapids, 1925.

13. Port Sheldon

"An Account of the Rapid Rise and Sudden Fall of Port Sheldon," *Michigan Pioneer Collections*. Vol. 28 (1898). p. 527.

History of Ottawa County, Michigan. Chicago, 1882.

Lillie, Leo C. *Historic Grand Haven and Ottawa County*. Grand Haven, 1931.

Meima, Ralph Chester. "A Forgotten City," *Michigan History Magazine*. Vol. V, Nos. 3-4 (July-October 1921). p. 379.

14. Wolves

Allen, Durward L. *Wolves of Minong.* Boston, 1979.

Burt, William H. *The Mammals of Michigan.* Ann Arbor, 1946.

Caesar, Gene. *The Wild Hunters.* N.Y., [1957].

Chips and Sticks. Battle Creek, 1886.

Clark, George. "Recollections," *Michigan Pioneer Collections.* Vol. 1 (1876). p. 501.

Mech, L. David. *The Wolves of Isle Royale.* Washington, 1966.

Osband, Melvin D. "My Recollections of Pioneers and Pioneer Life in Nankin," *Michigan Pioneer Collections.* Vol. 14 (1889). p. 431.

Utley, H.M. "Plymouth," *Michigan Pioneer Collections.* Vol. 1 (1876). p. 444.

Whitmore, O.S. "Treed by Wolves," *Outing.* March 1909.

15. Douglass Houghton

Allen, R.C. "Dr. Douglass Houghton," *Michigan Pioneer Collections.* Vol. 39 (1915). p. 124.

Bradish, Alvah. *Memoir of Douglass Houghton.* Detroit, 1889.

Carter, James L. and Rankin, Ernest H., eds. *North to Lake Superior: The Journals of Charles W. Penny 1840.* Marquette, 1970.

Fuller, George N., ed. *Geological Reports of Douglass Houghton 1847-1845.* Lansing, 1928.

Hubbard, Bela. *Memorials of a Half-Century.* N.Y., 1887.

Peters, Bernard C., ed. *Lake Superior Journal.* Marquette, 1983.

Wallin, Helen. *Douglass Houghton: Michigan's First State Geologist.* Michigan Geological Survey Pamphlet No. 1. Lansing, 1970.

16. Angelique

Duffield, George. *Angelique: A story of Lake Superior.* Sault Ste. Marie, [1892].

Holbrook, Stewart H. *Iron Brew: A Century of Iron and*

Steel. N.Y., 1939.

Nute, Grace Lee. *Lake Superior.* Indianapolis, [1944].

Swineford, A.P. *History and Review of the Copper, Iron, Silver, Slate and Other Material Interests of the South Shore of Lake Superior.* Marquette, 1876.

Williams, Ralph D. *The Honorable Peter White.* Cleveland, [1905].

17. Potters

Potter, Theodore Edgar. *Autobiography of.* [Concord, N.H., 1913].

Strange, Daniel. *Pioneer History of Eaton County, Michigan.* [Charlotte], 1923.

Wright, Ruth Lovell. *The History of Potterville, Michigan 1869-1976.* Potterville, [1977].

18. Laura Haviland

Dietrich, Emily. "Laura Smith Haviland: Emancipator," in *Historic Women of Michigan: A Sesquicentennial Celebration.* Edited by Rosalie Riegle Troester. Lansing, [1987].

Harris, Fran. *Focus: Michigan Women 1701-1977.* N.P., [1977].

Haviland, Laura S. *A Woman's Life—Work.* Cincinnati, 1881.

19. Mary Day

Day, Mary L. *Incidents in the Life of a Blind Girl.* Baltimore, [1859].

Fuller, George N., ed. *Michigan: A Centennial History of the State and its People.* 5 Vols. Chicago, 1939.

Mayhew, Ira. *Reports of the Superintendent of Public Instruction of the State of Michigan For the Years 1855, 56, 57...* Lansing, 1858.

20. Nessmuk

Kirk, John Foster. *A Supplement to Allibone's Critical Dictionary of English Literature...* 2 Vols. Philadelphia, 1891.

Romig, Walter. *Michigan Place Names.* Detroit, 1986.

Sawyer, Charles Winthrop. *Our Rifles*. Boston, 1941.

[Sears, George W.] *Woodcraft*. 12th ed. N.Y., 1900.

21. Daniel B. Kellogg

Kellogg, D.B. *Autobiography of*. Ann Arbor, 1869.

Stevens, Wystan. "A Man of Clear Vision: Dr. Daniel B. Kellogg, the Clairvoyant Physician," *Chronicle*. Vol. 13, No. 3 (Fall 1977). p. 4.

22. Pauline Cushman

Dictionary of American Biography. 21 Vols. N.Y., 1943.

Faust, Patricia L., ed. *Historical Times Illustrated Encyclopedia of the Civil War*. N.Y., 1986.

Moore, Frank. *Women of the War; Their Heroism and Self Sacrifice*. Hartford, 1867.

Rickman, Irwin. "Pauline Cushman. She Was a Heroine But Not a Lady," *Civil War Times Illustrated*. February 1969. p. 39.

Sarmiento, F.L. *Life of Pauline Cushman, the Celebrated Union Spy and Scout*. Philadelphia, [1865].

23. Battle of Tebb's Bend

Duke, Basil W. *Morgan's Cavalry*. N.Y., 1906.

Faust: *Encyclopedia of the Civil War*.

Holland, Cecil Fletcher. *Morgan and His Raiders*. N.Y., 1942.

Lanman, Charles. *The Red Book of Michigan*. Detroit, 1871.

Robertson, Jno. *Michigan in the War*. Lansing, 1882.

Travis, B.F. *The Story of the Twenty-Fifth Michigan*. Kalamazoo, 1897.

24. Libby Prison

[Durant, Samuel]. *History of Kalamazoo County, Michigan*. Philadelphia, 1880.

Faust: *Encyclopedia of the Civil War*.

Record of Service of Michigan Volunteers in the Civil War: Eighth Cavalry. [Kalamazoo, 1903].

Wells, James M. *"With the touch of Elbow" or Death Before Dishonor*. Philadelphia, 1909.

25. Bloomers

Carson, Gerald. *Cornflake Crusade.* N.Y., [1957].

Furnas, J.C. *The Americans: A Social History of the United States.* N.Y., [1969].

Massie, Larry B. and Schmitt, Peter. *Battle Creek: The Place Behind the Products.* [Woodland Hills, Cal., 1984].

Quaife, Milo M. *The Kingdom of St. James.* New Haven, 1930.

White, Ellen G. *Testimonies For the Church.* Battle Creek, N.D.

_____. "The Dress Reform. An Appeal To the People in Its Behalf," *The Health Reformer.* Vol. 3, No. 2. p. 1.

Willard, Frances E. and Livermore, Mary A. *A Woman of the Century.* Buffalo, 1893.

26. Philo Parsons

Ayer, Winslow I. *The Great Treason Plot In the North During the War.* Chicago, [1895].

Catlin: *Detroit.*

Hatcher: *Lake Erie.*

Horan, James D. *Confederate Agent: A Discovery in History.* N.Y., [1954].

Robertson: *Michigan In the War.*

Thorndale, Theresa. *Sketches and Stories of the Lake Erie Islands.* Sandusky, 1898.

Woodford, Frank B. *Father Abraham's Children: Michigan Episodes in the Civil War.* Detroit, 1961.

27. Fayette

Brooks, T.B., Pumpelly, Raphael and Rominger, C. *Geological Survey of Michigan: Upper Peninsula.* Vol. 1. N.Y., 1873.

Dunathan, Clint. "Fayette," *Michigan History.* Vol. 41, No. 2 (June 1957). p. 204.

History of the Upper Peninsula of Michigan. Chicago, 1883.

Jacques, Thomas Edward. *A History of the Garden Penin-*

275

sula. Iron Mountain, 1979.

Langille, James J. *Snail-Shell Harbor.* Boston, [1870].

Rosentreter, Roger L. "Delta County," *Michigan History.* Vol. 65, No. 5 (Sept./Oct. 1981). p. 9.

28. Bump Master

Andrews, Thomas S. *Ira Andrews & Ann Hopkinson Their Ancestors and Posterity...* Toledo, 1879.

Fowler, O.S. and L.N. *New Illustrated Self-Instructor in Phrenology and Physiology...* N.Y., 1859.

29. Coveney Monument

Berrien County Record. 1873-1874.

History of Berrien and VanBuren Counties, Michigan. Philadelphia, 1880.

Myers, Robert C. *Historical Sketches of Berrien County.* [Berrien Springs, 1988].

30. Pig Boats

Dowling, Edward J. "The Story of the Whaleback Vessels and of Their Inventor, Alexander McDougall," *Inland Seas.* Vol. 13, No. 3 (Fall, 1957). p. 172.

Elliott, James L. *Red Stacks Over the Horizon: The Story of the Goodrich Steamboat Line.* Grand Rapids, [1967].

Eniberg, R.A.E.M. *Phantom Caravel.* Boston, 1948.

Lydecker, Ryck. *Pigboat...The Story of the Whalebacks.* Duluth, 1973.

Mason, George Carrington. "McDougall's Dream: The Whaleback," *Inland Seas.* Vol. 9, No. 1 (Sept. 1953). p. 3.

Wilterding, John H., Jr. *McDougall's Dream: The American Whaleback.* [Green Bay, 1969].

31. River Hog

Whiting, Perry. *Autobiography of.* Los Angeles, [1930].

Foehl, Harold M. and Hargreaves, Irene M. *The Story of Logging the White Pine in the Saginaw Valley.* [Bay City, 1964].

32. Lyman E. Stowe

Record of Service of Michigan Volunteers in the Civil War.

Second Michigan Infantry. [Kalamazoo, 1903].
Stowe, Lyman E. *Poetical Drifts of Thought or Problems of Progress.* Detroit, 1884.
The Book of the Golden Jubilee of Flint, Michigan. 1855-1905. N.P., [1905].
33. Turkeys
Barrows, Walter Bradford. *Michigan Bird Life.* Lansing, 1912.
Block, John. "New Math Works for Turkeys," *Kalamazoo Gazette.* 12 March 1989.
Cook, A.J. *Birds of Michigan.* Michigan Agricultural Experiment Station Bulletin 94 (April 1893).
Hubbard: *Memorials of a Half-Century.*
Judd, Sylvester D. *The Grouse and Wild Turkeys of the United States, and Their Economic Value.* USDA Biological Survey Bulletin No. 24. Washington, 1905.
Mershon, William B. *Recollections of My Fifty Years Hunting and Fishing.* Boston, 1923.
Mosby, Henry S. & Handley, Charles O. *The Wild Turkey in Virginia: Its Status, Life History and Management.* Richmond, Virginia, 1943.
State of Michigan. *Game and Fish Laws.* Lansing, 1903.
Tibbits, John S. "Wild Animals of Wayne County," *Michigan Pioneer Collections.* Vol. 1 (1876). p. 403.
"Wild Turkeys Released in Northeast VanBuren County," DNR News Release, 1988.
34. George Shiras
Rydholm, C. Fred. *Superior Heartland: A Backwoods Story.* 5 Vols. in 2. Ann Arbor, 1989.
Shiras, George. "The Wild Life of Lake Superior, Past and Present," *National Geographic Magazine.* Vol. XL, No. 2 (August 1921). p. 113.
_____. *Hunting Wild Life With Camera and Flashlight.* 2 Vols. Washington, [1935].
35. Harry Smith
Portrait and Biographical Album of Osceola County,

Mich... Chicago, 1884.

Smith, Harry. *Fifty Years of Slavery in the United States of America.* Grand Rapids, 1891.

36. Chicora

Appleyard, Richard, ed. *Images of the Past.* South Haven, 1984.

Bowen, Dana Thomas. *Shipwrecks of the Lakes.* Daytona Beach, Florida, 1952.

Caesar, Pete. *Chicora.* Green Bay, Wisc., 1982.

Holland Daily Sentinel. 17 April 1917. p. 1.

Morton, J.S. *Reminiscences of the Lower St. Joseph River Valley.* [St. Joseph, N.D.]

37. Anna Howard Shaw

Giel, Dorothy and Lawrence. "Anna Howard Shaw: Orator," in *Historic Women of Michigan: A Sesquicentennial Celebration.* Edited by Rosalie Riegle Troester. Lansing, [1987].

Portrait and Biographical Album of Mecosta County, Mich... Chicago, 1883.

Shaw, Anna Howard. *The Story of a Pioneer.* New York, 1915.

Willard and Livermore: *A Woman of the Century.*

38. Grand Junction Saints

Byrum, Enoch E. *Travels and Experiences in Other Lands.* Anderson, Indiana, 1905.

_____. *Divine Healing of Soul and Body.* Grand Junction, 1892.

Kalamazoo Semi-Weekly Telegraph. 6 July 1898.

Indiana: A Guide to the Hoosier State. N.Y., 1941.

39. James D. Elderkin

Cyclopedic Review of Current History. Vol. 7 (1897).

Elderkin, James D. *Biographical Sketches and Anecdotes of a Soldier of Three Wars.* Detroit, 1899.

Florida: A Guide to the Southernmost State. N.Y., 1939.

Grant, Bruce. *America Forts: Yesterday and Today.* N.Y., [1965].

Lewis, Lloyd. *Captain Sam Grant*. Boston, 1950.
Morris, Richard D., ed. *Encyclopedia of American History*. N.Y., [1953].
Palmer Friend. *Early Days in Detroit*. Detroit, [1906].
Record of Service of Michigan Volunteers in the Civil War: First Michigan Infantry. [Kalamazoo, 1903].
40. James D. Corrothers
Corrothers, James D. *In Spite of the Handicap*. N.Y., [1916].
_____. *Selected Poems*. [South Haven, 1907].
Kerlin, Robert T. *Negro Poets and Their Poems*. Washington, [1923].
41. Caroline Bartlett Crane
Brown, Alan. "Caroline Bartlett Crane and Urban Reform," *Michigan History*. Vol. LVI, No. 4 (Winter, 1972). p. 287.
Dunbar: *Kalamazoo*.
Massie, Larry B. and Schmitt, Peter J. *Kalamazoo: The Place Behind the Products*. [Woodland Hills, Cal., 1981].
Rickard, O'Ryan. "Caroline Bartlett Crane: Minister to Sick Cities," in *Historic Women of Michigan: A Sesquicentennial Celebration*. Edited by Rosalie Riegle Troester. Lansing, [1987].
Schmitt, Peter. *Kalamazoo: Nineteenth-Century Homes in a Midwestern Village*. [Kalamazoo, 1976].
Willard and Livermore: *A Woman of the Century*.
42. Ring Lardner
Diedrick, James. "Ring Lardner's Michigan," *Michigan History*. Vol. 69, No. 2 (March/April 1985). p. 32.
Elder, Donald. *Ring Lardner*. N.Y., 1956.
Kunitz, Stanley J. and Haycraft, Howard. *Twentieth Century Authors*. N.Y., 1942.
Lardner, Ring. *Some Champions*. N.Y., [1976].
Lardner, Ring, Jr. *The Lardners: My Family Remembered*. N.Y., [1976].
Tobin, Richard L. "Ring Lardner, the Man With the Per-

fect Pitch," *Chronicle*. Vol. 14, No. 1 (Spring 1978). p. 11.

Yardley, Jonathan. *Ring: A Biography of Ring Lardner*. N.Y., [1977].

43. Good Roads

Dunbar, Willis. *Michigan: A History of the Wolverine State*. Grand Rapids, [1965].

Earle, Horatio Sawyer. *The Autobiography of "By Gum" Earle*. Lansing, 1929.

Fuller: *Michigan*.

Mason, Philip P. "Horatio S. Earle and the Good-Roads Movement in Michigan," *Papers of the Michigan Academy of Science, Arts, and Letters*. Vol. XLIII (1958). p. 269.

Stoddard, Asa H. *Miscellaneous Poems*. Kalamazoo, 1880.

Ziegler, Charles M. "Dedication Talk," *Michigan History*. Vol. 35, No. 1 (March 1951). p. 99.

44. David Grayson

Baker, Ray Stannard. *Native American: The Book of My Youth*. N.Y., 1941.

Bannister, Robert C. *Ray Stannard Baker: The Mind and Thought of a Progressive*. New Haven, 1966.

Dyer, Walter A. *David Grayson: Adventurer*. Garden City, 1926.

Grayson, David. *The Friendly Road*. Garden City, 1913.

Rand, Frank Prentice. *The Story of David Grayson*. Amherst, 1963.

45. Soper Frauds

Cumming, John. "Humbugs of the First Water: The Soper Frauds." *Michigan History*. Vol. 63, No. 2 (March/April 1979). p. 31.

Etzenhouser, Rudolph. *Engravings of Prehistoric Specimens From Michigan, U.S.A.* Detroit, 1910.

Kelsey, Francis. "A Persistent Forgery," *The Nation*. Vol. 90 (June 16, 1910). p. 603.

_____. "Archeological Forgeries at Wyman, Michigan," *The Nation*. Vol. 54 (28 Jan. 1892). p. 71.

_____. "Some Archeological Forgeries From Michigan" *American Anthropologist*. Vol. 10 (Jan.-March 1908). p. 48.

46. L. Frank Baum

Baum, Frank Joslyn and MacFall, Russell P. *To Please a Child: A Biography of L. Frank Baum, Royal Historian of Oz*. Chicago, 1961.

Baum, L. Frank. *Ozma of Oz*. Chicago, [1907].

Hearn, Michael Patrick, ed. *The Annotated Wizard of Oz*. N.Y., [1973].

Kunitz and Haycraft: *Twentieth Century Authors*.

47. Metz Fire

Johnson, Clifton. *Highways and Byways of the Great Lakes*. N.Y., 1911.

Micketti, Gerald. "The Day Metz Burned," *Michigan History*. Vol. 65, No. 5 (Sept./Oct. 1981). p. 12.

[Nagel, Herbert], ed. *The Metz Fire of 1908*. [Rogers City], N.D.

48. Aerial Elopement

Hillsdale Area Centennial 1869-1969. N.P.

Hillsdale Daily. 28 Oct. 1912, 30 Oct. 1912.

Scamehorn, Howard L. *Balloons to Jets*. Chicago, 1957.

49. The Big Blow

Barcus, Frank. *Freshwater Fury*. Detroit, 1960.

Bowen: *Lore of the Lakes*.

Boyer, Dwight. *True Tales of the Great Lakes*. N.Y., [1971].

Havighurst, Walter. *The Long Ships Passing*. N.Y., 1942.

Landon, Fred. *Lake Huron*. Indianapolis, [1944].

50. Red Arrow Men

Gansser, Emil B. *History of the 126th Infantry...* Grand Rapids, [1920].

Landrum, Charles H., compiler. *Michigan In the World War*. N.P., [1924].

Morris: *Encyclopedia of American History*.

Stallings, Laurence. *The Doughboys: The Story of the*

A.E.F., 1917-1918. N.Y., [1963].
The 32nd Division In the World War 1917-1919. [Milwaukee, 1920].
51. Thomas E. Dewey
Hughes, Rupert. *The Story of Thomas E. Dewey Attorney for the People.* N.Y., 1944.
Smith, Richard Norton. *Thomas E. Dewey and His Times.* N.Y., [1982].
"Tom Dewey Dies At 68," *Kalamazoo Gazette.* 17 March 1971.
52. State Office Fire
Carver, Carlisle. *Lansing's Biggest Fire.* N.P., [1951].
"State Office." Clippings File. State of Michigan Archives.
Wiskemann, Geneva K. Telephone Interview. 2 April 1989.

INDEX

283

288

Okemos, Chief, 62
Oklahoma, 200
Old Wing Mission, 64
Olivet College, 217
Oregon, 69
Osband, William, 79
Osceola County, 192
Otsego, 64
Ottawa, tribe, 15, 17, 20, 21, 25-27, 44, 45, 53, 54, 62-65, 109
Ottawa County, 62-68, 71-75, 123
Ottawa House, 71-75
Ourcq River, 256
Owen, Robert, 132
Owosso, 259-262
Owosso, Chief, 62

P

Pacific Ocean, 16, 17
Paine, Thomas, 153
Palo Alto, Battle of, 201
Panama, Isthmus of, 202
Panic of 1837, 63, 70, 74
Paris, 191
Paris World Exposition, 178
Parkman, Francis, 22
Pearl, Joseph F., 186
Peninsula Railroad, 143
Pennsylvania, 26, 27, 152, 174
Perrysburg, Ohio, 36
Pershing, John, 255
Petosky, Chief, 62
Pewamo, Chief, 62
Philadelphia, 73, 117, 138, 215
Phillips, John S., 227
Philo Parsons, ship, 137-140
Pigeon Creek, 72, 73
Pine Lake, 163
Pingree, Hazen, 203
Piqua, Ohio, 26

Pittsburgh, Pennsylvania, 25, 176
Pittsfield Township, 113
Plainwell, 64
Plough, George, 252
Plymouth, 80
Plymouth Colony, 172
Pokagon, Chief, 62
Poncho Villa, 255
Pontiac, 147
Pontiac, Chief, 19-23, 62
Pontiac's Rebellion, 20-23, 28
Port Huron, 73, 74, 219, 222, 252, 257
Port Sheldon, 71-75
Port Sheldon Co., 72-75
Portage Lake, 251
Posen, 243
Potawatomi, tribe, 27, 54
Potter, Diana, 92, 95
Potter, Theodore E., 91-95
Potterville, 92
Presque Isle County, 240-243
Proctor, Henry, 37, 38

Q

Quakers, 97-99
Quebec, 14, 17, 28, 55

R

Raisin Township, 98
Ransom, Epaphroditus, 123
Reed City, 180, 183
Reese, 171, 172
Reims, France, 257
Rensselaer Polytechnic School, 83
Resaca de la Palma, Battle of, 201
Revolutionary War, 23, 25, 28, 31, 53
Richland, 64

Larry B. Massie is a Michigan product and proud of it. Born in Grand Rapids in 1947, he grew up in Allegan. Following a tour in Viet Nam as a U.S. Army paratrooper, he worked as a telephone lineman, construction laborer, bartender and in a pickle factory before earning three degrees in history from Western Michigan University.

He honed his research skills during an eight-year position with the W.M.U. Archives and Regional History Collection. He left in 1983 to launch a career as a freelance historian, specializing in the heritage of the state he loves. An avid book collector, he lives with his wife and workmate Priscilla, and their 30,000 volume library, in a one room schoolhouse nestled in the Allegan State Forest. Sons, Adam, Wallie and Larry Jr., as well as a border collie named Maggie, and Jiggs, a huge saffron-colored feline, insure there is never a dull moment.

Larry and Priscilla Massie donned period costumes for their Celebrate the Great Lakes Chautauqua performances in 1989. (Photo courtesy Kalamazoo Gazette - Robert Maxwell, photographer)